Rose Hawthorne:

The Pilgrimage of Nathaniel's Daughter

Other Books by
Arthur and Elizabeth Odell Sheehan

Pierre Toussaint
Father Damien and the Bells

Rose Hawthorne

The Pilgrimage of Nathaniel's Daughter

by

Arthur and Elizabeth Odell Sheehan

ILLUSTRATED BY NORMAN SASOWSKY

VISION BOOKS

Farrar, Straus & Cudahy   *New York*
Burns & Oates   *London*

VISION BOOKS
IS A DIVISION OF
FARRAR, STRAUS & CUDAHY, INC.
PUBLISHED SIMULTANEOUSLY IN CANADA BY
AMBASSADOR BOOKS, LTD., TORONTO.
MANUFACTURED IN THE U.S.A.

RL–1911

To Alice

CONTENTS

CONTENTS

AUTHORS' NOTE

The story of Rose Hawthorne is a story of
mystery. The facts about her are easy enough
to find. She belonged to one of America's most
noted families. Many books have been written
about her, her famous father, Nathaniel Hawthorne, and the New England historical background from which they came.

Yet the more we read, the less simple Rose's
story grows. An unseen thread seems to run
through it. Surrounding it is an aura of mystery which the authors have been able only to
suggest here.

It would take much space to list all the books
and other sources consulted in writing this
story. Among them were Rose's own journals
and her biography of her father, *A Fire was
Lighted* by Theodore Maynard (Milwaukee:
Bruce), *Sorrow Built a Bridge* by Katherine
Burton (New York: Longmans, Green),
Mother Alphonsa by James J. Walsh (New

York: Macmillan), various magazine articles, and Rose's own publication *Christ's Poor*.

We wish especially to thank Moira Walsh, daughter of the late Dr. James J. Walsh, for very kindly lending us many letters her father had received from Rose Hawthorne. Thanks are also due to Reverend Mother Siena, O.P., of Rosary Hill, for sending us pictures.

FOREWORD

The name of Hawthorne, or Hathorne as it was then spelled, was known in America from the time the first ships bearing Puritan settlers sailed from England under the charter of the Massachusetts Bay Colony.

Several of these early Hawthornes distinguished themselves in strange ways: one took the lead in driving Quaker Ann Hutchinson from New England; another was a judge in the infamous witchcraft trials.

The latter was John Hawthorne, tall, stern, and dark-browed. He was a soldier, lawmaker, and judge. He commanded respect as he strode down the streets of Salem village in his black Puritan cloak and high-crowned hat.

When the witchcraft madness came in 1692, John Hawthorne was called to the meeting-house to take part in the trials. There was never a doubt in his mind that anyone accused of being a witch must die, and quickly too!

Some people said that one of the ill-fated women had looked with terrible blame upon Judge Hawthorne who stood staunchly, his Bible and sword by his side, to watch her led to Gallows Hill. But later, when the townsfolk saw the tragic errors of those days and prayed publicly for forgiveness, no one saw John Hawthorne bend a knee!

No wonder, some thought, the Hawthorne family fortunes began to fail after that. The men gave up their prosperous farms and took to the sea, silent, lonely, often visited by moods bleaker than the bleakest waters. The Hawthorne women, notably beautiful, sensitive and refined, stayed behind slightly dusty curtains in their down-at-heel Salem houses, waiting for the seafarers and seldom mingling in the social life of their neighbors.

Generations passed and the Hawthorne "curse" became a legend. Then came a Hawthorne who refused to go to sea. He dreamed instead of becoming a writer of books. This was Nathaniel.

A wonderful storyteller, Nathaniel Hawthorne was strangely haunted by the family traditions. Again and again that dark past seemed to cast weird shadows over the pages he was writing. The idea of sin and its effects upon fathers and sons fascinated him. He wrote many tales about it. In and out of his stories queer beings—ghosts, witches—floated in the dim light. Often, he said, as he sat writing in the old house in Salem, he thought he felt a mysterious spirit pass his door!

He never became a regular church member. The cold formal New England religion did not appeal to him. He couldn't forget the dreadful things that had been done in the Salem meeting-house so long ago. He could never believe in a Puritan God who would command men to persecute one another as his ancestors had done.

Yet he was aware of the world of the spirit and it always troubled him. The redeeming power of suffering, the hidden bond that draws all men together, the victory of love and mercy over justice and righteousness—how could these be explained? He felt in some way personally responsible for John Hawthorne's misdeeds, but how could he set those far-off events right and drive away that ghost forever?

All his life Nathaniel Hawthorne searched for the answers. He hardly knew what he was seeking, or where he would find it. In the end, it was left for another to take up and finish the mysterious pilgrimage.

This was Rose, his youngest daughter, whose story we tell here.

CHAPTER ONE

The Miraculous Pitcher

"Daddy! Daddy!" cried Julian, throwing the door of his father's study wide open. Nathaniel Hawthorne looked up in surprise.

"Come out in the yard, quick, Daddy! The baby's starting to walk!"

Mr. Hawthorne stood up, leaving the page he had been writing unfinished on the little desk. It was really too hot to work this after-

noon, anyhow, he thought, as he smilingly followed his six-year-old son out of the house.

He was just in time to see the youngest of
the Hawthornes suddenly lose her balance and
sit down in the middle of the lawn. Julian
laughed loudly, while his older sister, Una, ran
to help Rose up again. Rose turned her head
and saw everyone's amusement. Her already
pink face turned several shades deeper and her
eyes flashed angrily. Pushing away Una's hand
impatiently, she scrambled to her feet by herself. Planting one chubby foot firmly on the
ground, she tried to stamp the other one angrily on the soft grass.

"She's mad because we laughed at her,"
Julian said. "Oh, there she goes again!"

Now she rolled around, crying furiously at
this second failure.

"That's Rosebud—she has a temper to match
her red hair," Mr. Hawthorne said.

"Grandmother Peabody should see her now,"
called his wife from her chair nearby.

Mr. Hawthorne nodded. "She'll soon be
hiking to Sleepy Hollow right along with the
rest of us. Say, how about a walk in the woods
right now? I'm through writing for today." He
turned to his wife. "You know, Sophia, this
political writing doesn't interest me very
much."

He was working on a biography of his college friend, Franklin Pierce, who had just been

nominated for President of the United States. They had attended Bowdoin together and the book was his way of helping Pierce win the election.

"I know you'd rather be writing a novel," Sophia Hawthorne agreed cheerfully. "But don't forget, this book may bring us good fortune. That is, if Mr. Pierce does become President, he'll surely want to reward you in some way."

"Maybe, but I really wonder if I would like another government job after working for three years in the Salem customhouse. I think I've had enough of political appointments."

"Daddy, you said you'd take us for a walk." Julian tugged at his father's arm. "Come on, let's go up the hill."

"You people go along," said Mrs. Hawthorne. "I'd like to finish this letter to my mother. Since she can't come down from Boston to visit us, I must write her all the news of the family. I want to tell her Rose took a walk in the yard today."

Mr. Hawthorne went over and gently swung the still-fuming Rose up on his broad shoulder. Her tears stopped instantly.

With lively Julian on one side and the more gentle and dignified eight-year-old Una on the other, Mr. Hawthorne started out. Even on a hot summer afternoon, it would be cool up there, under the shady trees. Julian and Una thought their father spent far too much time writing stories and not nearly enough taking them for rambles through the Massachusetts countryside. Usually he spent the first part of the day shut up in his workroom, sitting before his little desk, covering many pages with big scrawly writing. The desk had funny faces on its tiny drawers, painted by Mr. Hawthorne to make the children smile.

Now Julian was running ahead, waving an imaginary sword and making thrusts at an unseen enemy. Una walked quietly beside her father. Rose, still perched atop Mr. Hawthorne's shoulder, waved delightedly to her mother as they all disappeared among the trees.

Mrs. Hawthorne watched them proudly. Although they had lived at Wayside only a short time, it already seemed like home to her. Yes, even its odd corners and slightly sagging gate were dear to her. She no longer felt that sense of dismay that had come when she first saw the old buff-colored house on Lexington Road.

"Oh, it's horrible," she had thought then. The farmhouse had been standing its ground staunchly since before the American Revolution. Paul Revere had passed very near it on his famous night ride in 1775. Only a short walk away stood the small wooden bridge where the farmers of Concord had met the British redcoats and fought them with muskets and pitchforks all the six miles to the next town of Lexington on a famous April day. All that seemed long ago. Now it was 1852, and Wayside—in fact, the whole peaceful town of Concord—seemed to dream in midsummer sun.

But Sophia Hawthorne was not a complaining person. Thanks to her artistic hands, Wayside was now very different. First she had fixed up her husband's study. It was most important that he have a pleasant place in which to work. With careful planning, for she had little money to spend for furnishings, she had bought the blue carpet. The paintings on the walls, the statue in the corner, the bowl of fruit on the table—all had been placed deftly to create the best possible effect. Mrs. Hawthorne was a talented painter herself and her pictures hung in many Boston homes.

She could still hear Rose's voice, shrill above the others, although the trees hid her from her mother's view. Rose was shouting in happy excitement, the pitfalls of learning to walk quite forgotten. One of the best things about Wayside, Mrs. Hawthorne thought, was the path that led up behind it to their backyard hill, with its birch, locust and pine trees in clusters. The Hawthornes were a walking family, and if they wanted to roam farther, they could cut across the yards and fields bordering the town and soon be at Walden Pond, or Sleepy Hollow, wading in marshlands, or sitting beside the peaceful Concord River.

Mrs. Hawthorne took up her pen and smoothed the sheet of paper that the breeze was gently ruffling. She must stop daydreaming and finish her letter to Grandmother Peabody quickly.

"I wish I could show you my Rosebud," she wrote, "She is wholly different from Una and Julian . . . inconceivably naughty and very bewitching." A constant stream of letters, describing everything that happened in both homes, flowed back and forth between Concord and Boston. The Peabodys were great letter-writers, and prominent educational leaders as well. Mrs. Peabody had a book store in West Street that was known as a cultural center. Sophia's sister Elizabeth opened the first kindergarten in America, while the third sister, Mary, became the wife of the noted educator and reformer Horace Mann.

In a few minutes the letter was finished and tucked into its envelope. Mrs. Hawthorne rose briskly from her garden chair. She was a small, neat, energetic person. The family would soon be back, tired and thirsty. She went in to fix them a cool drink.

When the summer months had passed and the leaves on the hill began to turn to autumn colors, Rose had become a sure-footed explorer of her small world. Keeping her out of trouble was enough to take up anyone's time, but Mrs.

Hawthorne had other plans too. Una and Julian were to attend "school" every day at the big round table in the dining room. Some of the other young people of the neighborhood came to the classes as well, for Mrs. Hawthorne was a wonderful teacher who could make any subject seem interesting. She would read to them from the Bible or some other great book, or tell them stories from her own wide knowledge. She herself could read easily in Italian, German, Hebrew, Greek and Latin.

One bright October afternoon Mrs. Hawthorne answered a knock at the door. It was Edward Emerson, son of Ralph Waldo Emerson, who lived nearby.

"Are you having class today?" he wanted to know.

"Yes, Edward. Come right in."

"Edith is coming over too. She was helping Dad out in the garden when I left," Edward explained. Edith was his older sister.

"Very well. I think Una and Julian are about ready to begin. As for you—" she hesitated and looked down at Rose who had come to the doorway, "do you want to come to school today too?"

Rose promptly answered by running over to the table and climbing up on one of the stiff-backed chairs.

Soon the others arrived and took their places

ready to begin. Just then there was a quick
loud rap at the back door.

"It must be Mr. Thoreau," said Mrs. Hawthorne as she rose to answer. She knew that
peculiar signal well, for the famous naturalist
was a frequent visitor to Wayside.

He strode into the room, looking a little
rough in his homespun coat and heavy boots.

"I'll call Nathaniel," said Mrs. Hawthorne.

"Don't bother," said her husband from the
hallway. "I heard your knock, Henry. What's
on your mind today?"

Without stopping for polite greetings, Thoreau spoke up gruffly.

"Thought I might take a walk over to
Walden and see how the pine trees are. Want
to come along?"

Henry Thoreau never had much to say, and
some might have thought his manners rude,
but those who knew him thought his brusque
speech was part of a very unusual and gifted
man.

Julian looked up, brightening. He would much
rather ramble with Mr. Thoreau than study at
home. His eyes turned to his mother and she
saw the question in them plainly.

"Do you want to go, Julian?" she asked.

Julian jumped up and ran for his jacket.
Thoreau clamped his broad hat down on his
head and turned to leave.

"Julian there—he's the naturalist all right.

What are you collecting now?" asked his father good-humoredly.

"Arrowheads, Dad. Remember, I showed you some."

"Think you can keep up with us?" asked Thoreau.

Nathaniel laughed. "You know no one can keep up with you, Henry."

"We were just in the midst of lessons," Mrs. Hawthorne explained to Thoreau as they walked to the door.

Her caller looked at her crossly. "You can learn more out in the woods than you can from books," he announced firmly. "Come now, let's get started."

When the three had gone, Mrs. Hawthorne turned back to her lesson. Rose, soon growing impatient, got down from her chair and began to play around the table.

"Mother," asked Una, "is that right, what Mr. Thoreau just said, that you can learn more from nature than from books?"

"Some people can," answered her mother. "He certainly does, but don't forget, he has also read books, even though he doesn't think too highly of them now."

"I don't understand it," said Una very seriously. "Daddy and Mr. Emerson write books, and Mr. Emerson says—" Mrs. Hawthorne smiled patiently as she listened to Una explaining Mr. Emerson's ideas on truth and beauty.

Why, the child sounded like the Sage of Concord himself! She certainly had absorbed many of his thoughts.

Una Hawthorne's friendship with the noted Mr. Emerson would have been a bit strange for most eight-year-olds, but not for grave and thoughtful Una, who often seemed much older than she really was.

Ralph Waldo Emerson, a former Unitarian minister, who had differed with his own church, made his living as a writer and lecturer. Then the country's most noted lecturer, his fervent mystical views held audiences spellbound, wrapt in a strange peace.

The Emersons often entertained and, though the children loved him, he awed them a little. One day, Una had gone to the Old Manse by herself.

"Come in, Una," said Mr. Emerson, greeting her at the door. "You've come over to see Edith perhaps?" His resonant voice was remarkably gentle and kind.

"No, Mr. Emerson, I came to see you." Una's pretty face was solemn and she held her head primly.

Concord's most famous citizen led his guest into his comfortable but shabby study. It wasn't often the Sage of Concord had callers this young!

"You know, Una," he said, "your father and mother once lived in this house. In fact, your father gave the place its name, the Old Manse, because so many ministers had lived here. He wrote his book *Mosses from an Old Manse* here. Right in this chair I'm sitting in now! Your father is a great writer, Una, a great man I think, and a deep one. Sometimes we have wonderful talks, when he's not too busy on his books."

"Oh, he's always busy on them!" Una said rather impatiently, tossing her dark red hair. "Too busy to play with us very much. But he does tell us good stories, and sometimes, after he tells them to us he writes them down for other children to read. That's how *The Wonder Book* came to be written."

Mr. Emerson smiled, a dreamy look in his half-closed eyes. Una looked at the awkward, somewhat bent figure. Mr. Emerson was anything but handsome, yet he seemed to have some magic about him that made her want to stay and talk to him more.

"What are you writing now, Mr. Emerson?" she asked finally. He reached for a sheaf of papers in a table drawer.

"Some pretty serious writing, Una. I don't think you'd find it as interesting as your father's tales. I call these essays, and they are about man's deep desire for beauty. Here, I'll read you a few lines if you like, but I won't mind if you get sleepy listening." He began to read the long sentences he had made up so carefully.

Una listened politely but she did not know exactly what it meant. Still Mr. Emerson's voice was so musical, his manner so sincere, she wished she knew more about it.

After that visit she returned often to the quiet study, learning more and more of what this man was trying to teach through his writing and speaking. She began to understand his thinking more and more, and when others questioned it in later years, she would always explain it clearly.

Winters in Concord were brisk and chill and there were many days when Una, Julian and Rose were glad to stay indoors, away from the swirling snowstorms and frigid winds. When the snow stopped, they would all bundle up in their warmest clothes and go out to tumble about in the high drifts. Mr. Hawthorne helped them build snow forts and sometimes took them to Walden Pond, now frozen over, for ice skating. Mr. Thoreau would often be there, cutting across the ice with awkward but expert speed and doing fancy figures that would have seemed very graceful done by anyone but him. Strong and sturdy Rose enjoyed rough games and did her best to keep up with the active Julian.

The end of the day was nearly always the

same. Everyone gathered in the living room and Mr. Hawthorne, leaning back comfortably in his old chair, told stories or read from a favorite book. This was the time Una and Julian looked forward to most. Even Rose loved to watch her father's handsome face as he talked. His broad brow and deep-set piercing eyes made him a commanding figure even in his own parlor.

"What shall it be tonight?" he would say, closing his eyes and pretending to be very tired.

"A story, please," Una would beg.

"Which story then?"

"*The Miraculous Pitcher*," suggested Julian, "from *The Wonder Book*."

"What? That old one again?" Mr. Hawthorne would feign surprise.

"Yes, we like it best of all," Una agreed. Then her father would read:

"One evening, in times long ago, old Philemon and his wife Baucis sat at their cottage door, enjoying the calm and beautiful sunset. . . ."

It was a story full of strange and wonderful happenings. Rose sat on her mother's lap and listened to her father's voice going on and on, telling how two strangers had come that evening to the old couple's cottage and had been received very kindly. Philemon and Baucis were poor, and though their hearts were gener-

ous, they had little in the way of supper to
offer their guests. Their small supply of bread
and milk quickly disappeared, but the pitcher
that stood on their plain table suddenly began
to fill itself with sweet fresh milk over and
over again. No matter how often it was poured
out, it was never empty, nor was the last piece
of bread ever eaten. Thus the wonder-working
strangers had rewarded the old couple for their
hospitality.

Rose's head was beginning to nod before the
story had ended but the sound of it went with
her as she fell asleep. Often again she would
hear this tale, and in the future *The Miraculous
Pitcher* was to have a strange meaning in her
own life.

CHAPTER TWO

Off to England

Mr. Hawthorne dropped wearily into his favorite old chair by the fireplace. He had just returned from Washington where he had visited President Franklin Pierce, his college friend. Hawthorne's book on Pierce had helped the latter to win the election. Now he felt tired, very tired, but so glad to be home in Wayside.

At first Rose had shyly hid her face from him, but now she climbed down from her mother's lap and solemnly placed her small hand in his to shake. She was nearing her second birthday.

"I guess she remembers me after all," said her father with a smile. "But, listen everyone, I have great news. President Pierce has appointed me American consul in Liverpool."

Julian jumped up excitedly. "You mean we're going to live in England, cross the ocean, and —and everything?"

"May I go over and tell the Emersons?" Una wanted to know.

Mrs. Hawthorne leaned forward, her eyes reflecting the great happiness she felt—first, at having her husband home once more, and then, at the prospect of going abroad, something she had always dreamed of doing.

"Oh Nathaniel, it's a great honor. Why, I hardly know what to say, but I'm—I'm so happy."

"I knew you would be, Sophia. It will be a great opportunity for us if we make the most of it. My salary will be much more than I could ever make by writing. It will pay for the children's education anyway."

Still holding Rose, he stood up and went to the window. The late afternoon sun lighted the new green of the grass and trees and showed clearly the little crooked path his feet had worn on his daily walks behind the house.

"Wayside will always be home," he told

them, "but it'll be good to see a bit of the world that lies beyond our hillside too." Rose watched her father as his face grew very serious and his wonderful deep-set eyes seemed to be looking at something far off.

"Besides," he went on thoughtfully, "this will give us a chance to visit our old homeland—perhaps to see the place where the English Hawthornes lived long before coming to America."

After the children had fallen asleep that night, full of plans for their trip abroad, Nathaniel and Sophia Hawthorne sat in the yellow lamplight and talked over the future. The consular appointment had come at just the right time for them. They could use the money, for the income from the sale of books—even popular books—was not very great. Perhaps they could even save something for the future.

It would be wonderful, Mrs. Hawthorne thought, for the children to see other countries. Plans were forming in her mind faster than she could count them. Perhaps they could visit Scotland too, and Wales, and the famous old cathedrals and art galleries. And there were France and Italy, with all their treasures of painting and sculpture.

"As for the job itself," said Mr. Hawthorne, "I don't know just what it will be like. But I do know one thing—it'll be a big change for me, after the quiet of my study here."

This was certainly true. He was known, even among his friends, as a rather silent man who spoke little and cared nothing for social affairs. In fact, some thought he was a bit too quiet. They felt there must be something mysterious about a man who spent most of his time either writing stories off in a room alone or walking by himself along the hill-path behind his home. But Sophia Hawthorne, who knew her husband's complex nature so well, felt that he would be a great success in the new work.

From then on, Una and Julian talked of nothing but the coming trip. Rose, not understanding what all the bustle and excitement meant, knew that something good was happening around her. Her second birthday came on May 20, in the midst of preparations for leaving Concord.

"Dr. Holmes wants me to come up to Boston Tuesday for dinner with him and some other friends," Mr. Hawthorne said one day. Any party with Oliver Wendell Holmes as host was sure to be gay, for the little doctor was as noted for his genial talk and literary wit as for his learned lectures in anatomy at Harvard.

"You've already promised Mr. Longfellow to have dinner with him next week," Mrs. Hawthorne reminded her husband.

"I know. I haven't time for all the dinners and farewell parties I'm invited to." Nathaniel Hawthorne laughed. The idea of going out so often amused him. It wasn't his usual habit at all.

At last the day of departure came. On the morning of July 6, 1853, the Hawthorne family went on board the *Niagara*, a steamship of the Cunard Line, in Boston harbor. As the ship weighed anchor they all stood on deck and watched the shores of America beginning to draw away from them.

"Here, Rose, wave good-by to Grandfather Peabody." Mr. Hawthorne held Rose high up so she could see Dr. Peabody smiling and waving to them from the pier. She hugged her father happily.

Just then the captain came along to greet them. "Welcome aboard the *Niagara!*" he said in a booming voice. "I hope you'll all have a very pleasant journey with us." He scanned the skyline. "If this fine weather holds, you'll enjoy every minute of it, I'm sure."

Mr. Hawthorne found himself quite at home on the ocean. Though this was his first long voyage, it did not seem like an altogether new experience to him. His father and grandfather had been Salem sea captains, one a stern commander, the other a melancholy rover of distant waters. He himself was the first of many Hawthorne sons who did not take to the helm. The

pen had held him too strongly, but his ambitions to be a writer had not taken away a
feeling for the sea and its ways.

On the calm and sunny days of the voyage,
Una and her mother sat on the deck, Una reading her father's *Tanglewood Tales* again, and
Mrs. Hawthorne talking with the other passengers.

Julian often went to stand beside his father
who liked to lean on the rail looking out over
the water with that peculiar distant look they
all knew so well.

"Daddy, tell me what you're thinking of,"
he asked one day.

Mr. Hawthorne went on gazing at the water
as he answered, "Why, Julian, just then I was
thinking of my father. How often he must
have stood watching the waves as we are doing
now!"

"Captain Hawthorne." Julian spoke his grandfather's name proudly. "What was he like,
Dad? Tell me about him."

Julian and the others had heard many wonderful stories from Mr. Hawthorne, but
strangely, he did not tell them much about his
own family. His early life in Salem seemed to
have a shadow, a sadness about it that he was
reluctant to recall.

"Well, Julian," he told his son now, "I never
knew my father very well. I was only four

years old when he caught the fever and died far
from home, in Surinam."

"Were his ships anything like this one?" Julian wanted to know.

"Not much. In his time all ships were sailing
vessels. Steam-driven ones like this came a little
later."

Suddenly the sun disappeared behind a cloud
and the water seemed to turn dull and gray.

"Was he afraid of storms at sea?" Julian
asked, looking up at his father a little anxiously.

"No, I think he rather liked storms, Julian.
He used to write in the ship's log descriptions
of his adventures and his thoughts. Some of his
notes were in rhyme. But the life of the sea was
hard, hard and lonely. He was never at home
very much, but he did manage to see a great
deal of the world—the West Indies, the Orient,
Europe—"

Mrs. Hawthorne had come to the railing in
time to hear the last part of the conversation.
She held Rose's hand firmly and tried to
smooth down the little girl's hair which the
sea breeze kept ruffling.

"Why not go and play cards with Una
now, Julian?" she suggested. "She's tired of
resting and wants a game."

That was her way of turning the talk to
brighter subjects. She did not like to have her
husband think too much about his years at
"Dismal Castle," as she always called the

Hawthorne home in Salem. She was adept at emphasizing the brighter side of life, and in this she helped her husband a great deal, for his moods were often tinged with sadness.

"Just think, Nathaniel," she said now, "in a few days we'll be there! This lovely trip will be over and we'll have all the art galleries of England before us."

Her eyes sparkled as she looked out over the restless water. She was full of plans and dreams for everyone.

"Yes, Sophia," replied her husband. "I think it's wonderful for you and the children." He himself welcomed the prospect of serving as American consul in England. It would be good to have a little more activity after the quiet years in America. And he had, in the back of his mind, another reason for going to England.

"I was thinking, Sophia," he continued, "maybe we could visit the place where the Hawthornes first lived before coming to the New World. I'd like to learn more about them. It would help me to understand——"

He did not finish the thought. He found it hard to explain exactly what his idea was in finding again his ancestral home. He turned abruptly and lifted Rose in his arms.

"What do you say, Rosebud? Shall I carry you downstairs now? That breeze is getting a bit stiff for you, isn't it?"

Soon the shores of their forefathers were upon them. As the steamer made its way up the Mersey River to Liverpool, the Sunday church bells rang all the way as if to welcome them.

CHAPTER THREE

The Hawthorne Tree

Across the broad Mersey River, not far from
the industrial city of Liverpool, the Hawthornes
had found a house at Rock Ferry. Those first
days in the damp and smoky city had made them
all a bit homesick for the clean and quiet streets
of Concord.

At Rock Ferry things were much more to
their liking. The important thing, at least
from Mrs. Hawthorne's viewpoint, was that

the two-story stucco villa had a big garden, a lawn, and plenty of room around it for the three young Hawthornes to play. And from the viewpoint of Fanny Wrigley, the kind English nurse who came to stay with the family, the important thing was that there were gooseberry bushes in the yard. That meant, to a true English heart, plenty of proper jam for tea!

To Rose, the most important thing turned out to be a flower, a small and simple English daisy that was to be hers long afterward in a very special way. There were many other flowers in that garden—purple violets and yellow laburnum—but Rose never forgot that daisy. Years afterward, she said it was the very first thing she could remember. Flowers were always important to her. Rose Hawthorne— the name itself was symbolic.

One Saturday afternoon in their first spring in England, Una, Julian and Rose were busy in the garden. Robins chirped cheerily on the new grass. The garden was newly spaded and three small sections had been marked off with stakes and string. These were to be flower beds for Una and Julian. Of course Rose too must try her hand.

"See, here's how you do it," Julian was explaining. With a broad stick he drew a little furrow in the fine soft earth. "Don't go down too far, or the seeds won't be able to grow."

Una was carefully dropping seeds in a straight line from a little package in her hand. "I know how to do it," she assured her brother. "I'm older than you."

"Me too," Rose piped up. Her plot was the smallest, and by the look of it, Julian's well-meant lesson in gardening had not done his small sister much good. She had drawn wavy lines here and there with a crooked twig.

"I'm ready. Give me some seeds now," she announced.

"Not that way!" Una exclaimed. "Julian, help Rose get hers fixed right. They'll never—" Just then something caught Una's attention, a bright and beady eye staring out from under the gooseberry bush. "Look, there's the rabbit again. He's watching us. He must live in our yard."

"Maybe he's wondering if we're planting anything he likes to eat," Julian laughed, jumping up to take a closer look at the watchful animal.

"Oh, you scared him away!" Una was disappointed. The tiny creature had nimbly jumped away to hide when he heard Julian's loud voice.

"When I was in 'Morica," said Rose wisely, rubbing a mud-smudged fist across her cheek, "rabbits weren't like that!"

"How would you know?" Una smiled. "You don't really remember America at all.

You're just pretending because you hear us talking about it so much."

"Oh yes, I do too," Rose insisted. She really felt she remembered Wayside very well.

"But she's right," Julian said. "At home the rabbits are larger, and not reddish-colored like this one." Julian always seemed to have the last word on matters like this. Nature and the outdoors were his special interest.

Just then Fanny came hurrying out of the house.

"It's company," she announced in a flurry. "Julian and Una, go in and wash your hands and faces." She turned to Rose and tried to wipe the child's face with a corner of her big apron. "Goodness, child, you *are* a sight!" She took Rose's grimy hand and hustled her into the house for a quick clean-up.

Company at Rock Ferry was not at all unusual, nor was Fanny's state of gentle confusion. Sometimes there were visitors from America or acquaintances Mr. Hawthorne had made in England. As consul, he had a certain number of official visitors, and when word got about that America's best known novelist was living for a time at Rock Ferry, the writers and literary people of England were anxious to meet him. Mr. Hawthorne himself had always been a rather retiring man. He did not even now go out of his way to make new friends, though he actually enjoyed social occasions more than before. Sometimes, as a visiting dignitary, he was even called upon to make speeches, and as he appeared very handsome, witty and at ease, no one guessed he might have preferred to sit quietly and listen to others do the talking.

No matter how busy Nathaniel Hawthorne might be with his official duties during the week, nothing was allowed to interfere with his Sunday custom of taking a walk with his children. This was the day Rose looked forward to most of all. They would ramble through the flower-bordered lanes and country roads around Rock Ferry, past picturesque whitewashed cottages with sturdy thatched roofs, past fields ruled off neatly with green hedges.

Not far away was Eastham, with its famous old yew tree that had stood for hundreds of years. It was the Hawthornes' favorite stopping place. Here Mr. Hawthorne would sit quietly, his back propped up against the giant trunk, puffing on his daily cigar and blowing the blue smoke thoughtfully into the still air. Una, Julian and Rose played house or other games of their own invention.

One day Julian, who had been exploring on his own a little way off, came running to his father.

"Look, Dad, see this flower. It's just like some we had at home in our garden, isn't it?"

Mr. Hawthorne took the delicate blue flower and studied it carefully.

"You're right, Julian," he said slowly. "This is a bluebell. And if those sharp eyes of yours are working, you'll see other flowers around here that look familiar."

"Yes, we've already found crocus—and primrose," Julian remembered.

"There are many others like them, all growing wild here in England."

"How come?" the ever-curious Julian wanted to know.

Rose ran up to listen to what they were saying. Whenever a story seemed likely to be told, Rose was always close at hand. She loved her father's stories. Now she waited expectantly, but her father asked a question instead.

"Well, Julian, how do you think it happens that we find the same flowers in New England as in old England?"

Una looked up from her book. "Did the English settlers bring them to America?"

"That's it, Una," said Mr. Hawthorne. "Under the charter of the Massachusetts Bay Colony, which had been granted by the King of England, each person was told exactly what food, clothing and other things to bring along on the ship. If there was a bit of space left over, it was often stuffed with seeds—partly to grow food, which was very scarce in the colony, and partly to have a little bit of the mother country with them in the wilderness."

He glanced down at the tiny blue flower already beginning to wither on the grass beside him. Like so many other things he saw in England, it reminded him strongly of his own ancestors, those brave adventurous Hawthornes who had first left their English homes to settle in Massachusetts. Wherever he went on his sight-seeing trips these days, Mr. Hawthorne seemed to see traces of these forefathers of his, but they were like messages written in code. He wished he could make more sense of them so that he could understand better the story of his own family, and especially those stiff Puritan beliefs that had made them so intolerant toward those of other faiths.

The dust of many ages lay over the Hawthorne secrets, yet their mysteries had a strange hold on him.

On the way home, Mr. Hawthorne took Rose's hand and led her to a small tree by the roadside. It was covered with pale pink fragrant blossoms. Mr. Hawthorne broke off a small branch and gave it to Rose.

"Look, this tree gave you your name—Hawthorne!" he told her.

Rose sniffed the delicate perfume and touched the fragile petals gently. Her eyes lighted up with the new, delightful discovery.

"Hawthorne?" She was surprised.

"Yes, and you know, Julian and Una, it was

these hawthorne blossoms that gave not only our name to us, but the name of the ship that brought the first settlers to Massachusetts—the Mayflower."

Rose held the branch tightly. "I'm going to take it home," she decided. Her mother must see it. And it reminded her of something she wanted to do as soon as she got home. She was going to dig up those seeds she had planted yesterday and see if they had started to grow yet!

"Where does Daddy go on the ferry every day?" Rose had asked her mother over and over.

At last Mrs. Hawthorne decided to take Rose to Liverpool and let her see for herself the office of the American consul. Mrs. Hawthorne did not care too much for the city, but she had some shopping to do before the family set out on a holiday trip to northern England and Wales.

As Rose and her mother boarded the small ferry early in the afternoon there were few other passengers, but the band was playing gaily just as if it were a holiday instead of a regular weekday afternoon. The lilting tunes made the two-mile crossing gay. Rose chattered brightly about the ships of many countries lying at anchor on the busy Mersey River. But when they reached the other side

and began to climb the steep staircase that led
to Mr. Hawthorne's office on Brunswick Street,
she began to complain.

"Why is it so dark here, Mama? Does
Daddy have to stay here all day?" she asked,
frowning.

They went down a shadowy hall and into
the cramped dark office. Rose looked sideways
at the roughly dressed men in the waiting
room.

"Who are they, Daddy?" she wanted to
know, as soon as she was inside.

"Don't let them frighten you, Rose," her
father smiled. "They are American sailors,
most of them, who come here for help.
They're rough-and-ready fellows, a little
weather-beaten perhaps, but harmless enough."

As he tried to reassure Rose, Mr. Hawthorne realized that he himself had felt hesitant
about talking to these men when he had first
come to Liverpool. It was his job, as American
consul, to look after the needs of American
seamen in the large port city. Many of them
were stranded without money when something
happened to their ships. Sometimes illness or
other trouble overtook them and Mr. Hawthorne had to supply emergency help for them
and their families. Many of their stories were
shocking and unpleasant at first to the sensitive author who had never before had much to
do with poverty and human suffering. Some-

times even after he left the office for his
pleasant home in Rock Ferry, he could not
easily forget the careworn faces and ragged
clothing of those he had met that day, and
their endless tales of trouble lay heavily on his
mind.

"Daddy, come home now and play with
me," Rose begged. "Don't stay here a minute
longer!"

"In a little while, Rosebud," he answered
gently. "Right now, I have some more work
to do."

They did not stay much longer. Rose was
glad to go down the dingy stairs and out again
into the street.

During their four years in England, the
Hawthornes took many trips. Mrs. Hawthorne
was a tireless sight-seer, and she did not intend
to leave a single place of historic or artistic
importance unvisited. She thought this was a
major part of the education of Una, Julian and
Rose. It was, in fact, a curious sort of school
for them. Instead of sitting in a classroom
studying literature, they visited the home of
Sir Walter Scott and saw the settings of his
adventure stories. Rather than learning some
lines of Tennyson, they followed the poet
himself through the galleries of the Manchester
Museum where his somber black-clad figure
suddenly loomed before them. Instead of maps

and geography books, they had the hills and
lanes of Wales to roam, as well as Scotland
and the Isle of Man. Mrs. Hawthorne, who
did not attend any church regularly, took
them to visit old cathedrals, showed them
stones worn smooth by the knees of the faithful, and the cold bare niches that had been,
before the Reformation, shrines of the Blessed
Virgin.

Mr. Hawthorne soon had to admit that his
enjoyment of museums and cathedrals was
very limited. Looking at picture after picture
hanging in a gallery often gave him a head-
ache and he would go outside for a walk and
some fresh air, leaving Mrs. Hawthorne and
the others inside with sketch books and pen-
cils. As he wandered around he was gathering
thoughts and impressions which he would later
record in his daily journal or in books. Julian
too was quickly bored by art and antiquities.
He had the habit of carrying his fishing line
in his pocket, and as soon as they arrived at
a new place he would head for the nearest
stream to try his luck.

Rose was still too young to understand
many of the things she saw, but she had her
own adventures. She was taken to see Tom
Thumb and the real Chinese junk anchored in
Liverpool harbor with its Oriental crew. There
were tales of giants and fairies, Druid circles
of stone, the Scottish gorse and honeysuckle

that she loved. She wondered why the cats on the Isle of Man had no tails and how the shells on English beaches were colored pink, and whether God had hurt Himself making a prickly crab.

Although she did not know it, her busy mind was storing up memories day by day. Often by night she would be too excited from the day's activities to go to sleep right away. Lying quietly in bed, her eyes closed tightly, her lively imagination would conjure up a fairy world all her own. Sometimes she saw faces of people, known and unknown. Among these, her father's face always stood out most clearly, handsomer than all the rest, a mystery in his eyes that she could not quite understand. It was a look she had noticed even when her father seemed most gay and carefree, playing boisterous games with her on rainy days indoors. She always meant to ask him if he was thinking of something sad, only she never found the right words for her question, and so it was never asked.

Outwardly at least, Mr. Hawthorne always treated misfortune as a joke or as something to be completely ignored. He tried both of these methods when the whole family came down with whooping cough, and though it helped a lot, it did not cure the coughs. Mrs. Hawthorne especially suffered from it, so much that she became quite ill and the doctor said her health was seriously threatened. It would be helpful for her to get away from the dampness of the English climate. Fortunately a letter soon came from Lisbon in sunny Portugal. It was from John O'Sullivan, Una's godfather, who had recently been appointed American ambassador at the Portuguese court.

"My wife and I would love to have you come and stay a while with us here," he wrote. "The weather is lovely and the change would be good for you. . . ."

The invitation was accepted gladly. Mrs. Hawthorne, Una and Rose left to spend a month in Portugal, and Julian stayed in England with his father.

Never had Rose, even in her colorful dream world, imagined such an adventure! To be welcomed by the King of Portugal and to play every day in the palace gardens—this did not happen to every small girl!

Even Mrs. Hawthorne was thrilled. She went to be presented to the king in her best white satin gown, with white feathers in her hair, and her dainty fan poised carefully in white-gloved hands.

"And what do you think?" she told Una and Rose excitedly after talking to His Majesty. "He asked me to give drawing lessons to one of the young princes!"

This was an honor the romantic Mrs. Hawthorne would always treasure. Rose thought

she had suddenly become a fairy-tale princess.
At any rate she took on a very royal manner
which could be sometimes trying and sometimes amusing to the palace servants. They
were not quite prepared for the small American girl who stood before them with angry
eyes and stamping foot, quite annoyed because,
being Portuguese, they had not understood her
American commands.

The parting from his family, although for
only a month, made Mr. Hawthorne lonely
and sad. He took a few days off from the
consulate and went with Julian to see the
sights of the great city of London.

The exploration of London, so thrilling to
a boy like Julian, often brought sadness to the
more observant eyes of his father. He was
terribly shocked by the slums. At the consulate he had for the first time met face to face
the hardships of the poor. But never had he
seen anything to compare with the dirty
streets with their rundown tenements and
haunting hungry faces.

One day Mr. Hawthorne was taken on a
tour of a poorhouse sheltering the homeless of
all ages. A little child, thin, deformed and
mentally deficient, kept tugging patiently at
the visitor's coat as he passed through one of
the dreary wards.

It was an effort for Mr. Hawthorne not to

yield to his first impulse to brush away the small clinging none-too-clean fingers from his well-pressed coat. But somehow the pathetic child's presence demanded attention. He could not speak plainly, yet he showed quite clearly he wanted to be picked up. Perhaps he wished just for a moment to feel that he belonged to someone, even if only a strange gentleman with a kindly look in his eyes.

"He's sure to go away in a minute," Mr. Hawthorne thought. He made a move to pass on to the next room. The child went right along with him. The pull of the small hand became more insistent. It seemed to have a sharpness, an urgency that could not be denied. Although it was certainly the last thing he felt like doing, Mr. Hawthorne bent over at last and lifted the poor child in his arms. A light burden, compared to the robust Rose he was used to carrying!

The child's smile was one of purest gratitude.

Late that night, after Julian, full of his day's adventures, had finally fallen asleep, Mr. Hawthorne sat at the small table in their room writing in his journal. The visit to the poorhouse occupied his mind. The eyes of the ragged child, his pleading hands, his look of gratitude came back full force as Mr. Hawthorne described the scene on the page before him.

Later, when there was leisure for writing,

many of these scenes would be used in books.
At any rate, this particular scene would never
be forgotten. Strangely enough, though Rose
was at that moment playing at being a princess in far-off Portugal, she too would keep
the memory of the nameless child who sym-
bolized for Nathaniel Hawthorne all the suffering of the poor.

CHAPTER FOUR

Adventures in Italy

Nathaniel Hawthorne sat shivering with cold in the large Rome apartment he had rented for their Italian stay. His work at Liverpool had ended and he had promised the family this visit to Italy as a treat before returning to America.

Outside his window, a frozen fountain stood watch in the stone-paved square. Sitting before the half-hearted fire on the hearth, he had felt much like that fountain for so many days. The visit was hardly a treat. Nor was the climate all he didn't like about the Eternal City! To begin with, he had never liked priests and monks. Here there was an almost steady stream of them past his window. He had expected to find a dead city, dignified and reverential, a mausoleum of a golden past. Instead, he found a city very much alive, teeming with beggars and street vendors, with tattered clothing hanging across broken monuments and everywhere an apparent indifference toward the glory that was Rome's.

Finally, the days began to soften and the pale sun turned warm and golden. It melted the icy fountain and blazed gloriously through the great windows of St. Peter's, flooding the inside with marvelous colored lights. Here, Hawthorne had to admit, time itself seemed to be nothing and the warmth of many ages of faith was added to that of the sun. Not even the hardest prejudice could hold before the beauty of the Roman spring.

At the very center of Rome, the spiritual city, was the mysterious figure of the Pope, a great Pope, Pius the Ninth. Pio Nono, the Italians called him. The Hawthornes felt his presence strongly and were curious about him.

Sometimes Mrs. Hawthorne took Rose to play in the Vatican gardens. This time she had brought her ball.

"One—two—three—four." She bounced and
counted and counted and bounced. Up and
down the ball went, till suddenly it hit a crack
and veered away from Rose. She dashed after
it in her exuberant way, headlong and swift.
Suddenly she collided with something. She
looked up, startled to find herself before a tall
white-clad man who smiled down at her
kindly. Rose pushed her tousled red hair out
of her eyes and looked hard at the strange
figure. Something in his pale face reassured
her. Pio Nono! Yes, it must be.

Mrs. Hawthorne was rushing forward to
apologize. The Holy Father brushed her em-
barrassment aside. He leaned over and put his
hand for a moment on Rose's head and blessed
her. Then he moved on, wrapped up once
more in deep thought.

Afterward, Rose asked her mother for a
keepsake of him. Mrs. Hawthorne bought her
a little medal and a gold coin bearing his
picture. To Rose, it seemed the image of a
friend.

Later they saw Pius the Ninth again, pray-
ing at St. Peter's one Friday night in Lent.
He was again dressed in white, this time with
a red mantle, red shoes, and a round white
cap. He blessed the crowd with a gesture that
surely meant to include all—even the non-
Catholic Hawthornes, and especially Rose. To
them the services seemed mysterious and very

solemn. At Tenebrae, Rose watched fascinated as the candles were extinguished one by one before the altar and a sad silence descended upon the congregation. She did not know what it was all about, but it had made a deep impression upon her.

Back home that night Rose's lively spirit at last rebelled against too much solemnity and sitting still. The others did not know whether to laugh or scold when Rose began to walk slowly around the room, as she had seen the monks in the procession, imitating in comic fashion the liturgical chants.

Mrs. Hawthorne reveled in the picturesque ruins and galleries of famous art works. Her husband, on the other hand, did not feel he had to see everything. His mind kept going back to one particular statue he had seen in the Villa Borghese. This was the Faun of Praxiteles, a rather odd figure, half-animal, half-human. The idea of such a mythical creature appealed to Mr. Hawthorne. It might be the seed of a story, a book about Rome that was slowly beginning to shape itself in his mind.

"I've finally arranged for our trip to Florence," Mr. Hawthorne announced one day. Rome would be sticky and uncomfortable during the summer, so the family planned to go farther north. "A driver says he'll take us for one hundred dollars. That includes meals and lodging on the way too."

They left early in the morning on a beautiful day in May. As the driver stowed away the luggage, the inevitable beggars crowded around the carriage. Their very evident misery offended Hawthorne, yet he could not be utterly cold to their pathetic pleas.

Down between the high brick walls of the old Flaminian Way they went, the driver urging his horses out into the hilly country. Here peasant women on horseback passed them and the road was dotted with wayside shrines, some with bunches of fading flowers around them.

In the town of Assisi, they paused to visit the church St. Francis had rebuilt. Village after village they passed through, Nathaniel Hawthorne's observant eyes taking note of everything. He was storing up material for stories he hoped to write by and by. Wherever they went in Italy, everyone seemed to be talking. "So many words are not spoken in a New England village in a whole year as here in this single day," he remarked.

At Perugia they went to see the statue of St. Rose of Lima in the Staffa Palace. Miss Elizabeth Hoar, a family friend, had told them they must not miss it because, she said, "That is Rose's patron saint." Rose knew nothing about patron saints, but she gazed for a polite length of time at the figure of the lovely young Peru-

vian girl who had lived in the far-off days of
the seventeenth century. At fifteen years of
age, Rose learned, she had received the white
habit of the Third Order of St. Dominic. She
was noted as the first canonized saint of the
Americas.

At Florence a thirteen-room house, Casa
Bello, awaited them, each room filled to over-
flowing with heavily carved furniture and elaborate draperies. Rose wandered disconsolately
through the old-fashioned villa and wondered
what she would ever find to do here. So lonely
and bored was she that it was a treat when a
short time later her mother took her to tea at
the home of one of the famous families then
living in Florence, the Brownings.

Rose had heard many tales of the jolly talka-
tive poet and his frail wife. Their son Pennini
was nine years old—an unusual child who
seemed neither very young nor very old. He
had a wise way of speaking and giving his
opinions, but Mr. Hawthorne had shaken his
head in a worried way when he saw that
Pennini was dressed in an embroidered silk
tunic. His mother was very proud of his long
curls. It was a strange life for a boy, but then,
nearly everything in the Browning household
was different!

All the way to the Brownings' Casa Guidi
Rose thought excitedly of the important meeting that was about to take place. But it was

not Mrs. Browning whom she looked forward to seeing. She had heard stories of another great Florentine named Galileo. For some reason she pictured Galileo in the back yard at Casa Guidi, peering through his newly invented telescope toward the sun. That Galileo had lived several hundred years before did not occur to Rose just then.

As they were ushered into the dim drawing room, Mrs. Browning came forward to greet them. She wore a dark velvet dress, and her sad pale face was lit up by a vivid smile. Her thin fingers grasped Rose's hand with a startling strength that belied her fragile appearance.

"Rose, how are you? Come here, dear."

Rose obediently sat on Mrs. Browning's lap.

"But where is Galileo?" she asked.

"Why, did you expect to see him here?" gasped Mrs. Browning.

Rose somehow felt cheated. The person she had really come to see wasn't there! The fact that she was sitting on the lap of the world's foremost woman poet did not mean much to her.

Later the Brownings arranged for Rose and her family to spend the month of August at a villa in the hills outside Florence called Montauto. Here it was a little cooler and one could escape from the sights and sounds of the city. Rose loved the old house which was something straight from a storybook. It even had a tower,

cracked and musty, with yellow moss covering
its gray stones. From the top you could look
down on the River Arno and the town of
Fiesole.

If Hawthorne wanted a quiet place for writing, Montauto was ideal! Some of the rooms
were so remote that no household sound could
possibly reach them. Here Rose's father began
to sketch out the opening chapters of his
Roman novel, *The Marble Faun.*

Montauto reminded Rose of a medieval castle,
with secret doors, an enchanted tower and
perhaps—who could tell?—a hidden treasure!
She tried to forget about Florence, for many
things she had seen there made her sad. Children no bigger than she was begged in the
streets, many of them crippled and deformed
beyond hope. Rose sensed ugliness and sorrow
everywhere. One day she had seen in the
Church of San Spirito an unforgettable scene,
the funeral of a child. She had watched them
carry in the small white casket as the choir
began the Mass of the Angels.

To her mother Rose said little about these
things. The only Catholic Rose knew very well
was Stella, the maid who helped take care of
her at Montauto. Stella was good and kind and
tried to answer all Rose's questions. She was
willing enough to explain everything, but she
could say very little. Stella's faith was of the
simple kind that is hard to put into words.

Rose knew that Stella prayed every day before a big black crucifix in her room.

The summer soon ended and it was time to say good-by to Montauto and its romantic tower. Before they left, Stella gave Rose a keepsake. It was a little glass case containing the figure of the Infant Jesus made of wax, sleeping on a bed of tiny flowers. In Rose's memories the little wax "bambino" stayed among her dearest treasures—a warm remembrance of faith and love.

This time as they entered Rome it was with a very different feeling from the first time. Now they all looked forward to the second visit. The deep booming of St. Peter's great bell every evening had a familiar sound.

Yet the shadow that was to fall over their second stay in Rome drew near quickly. In November the warm bright days gave way once more to the damp gray weather. Chill winds played among the ancient ruins. Coldness seemed to pierce everything.

One morning Una awoke feeling ill and feverish. "She must have stayed out too long at the Palace of the Caesars," said her mother. Una and her tutor had gone there in the early afternoon to make sketches of the ruins, and without their noticing it, the weather had turned very cold. They had both been shivering when they came home.

Una's sickness did not respond to Mrs. Hawthorne's trusted remedies. The doctor came. He seemed worried.

"It's Roman fever," he told them. He suggested various medicines but none seemed to help. Una grew weaker. Days passed and Mrs. Hawthorne hardly left the bedside. At last the doctor gave up the case, saying there was no hope.

There was nothing they could do now but wait. The terrible strain had begun to tell on everyone in the family. Each day Nathaniel Hawthorne's friend, former President Pierce, came to spend a little while. He happened to be staying in Rome, and as he had recently lost his only son in an accident he understood just how Mr. Hawthorne was feeling. Everyone was very helpful and sympathetic, but no one could do what was needed most. Una, worn out by weeks of fever, had not much strength left. Even Mrs. Browning, who seldom left her own home, came each day to call, bringing little delicacies for Una.

For the first time in her life Rose had her father all to herself each day. He took her to the Pincian Hill overlooking the city, where Roman emperors of old had had their magnificent gardens. She would sit beside him on the marble seat looking out over the city built on seven hills. The great dome of St. Peter's stood out sharply against the blue Mediterranean sky. Mr. Hawthorne's eyes looked dreamy as he gazed out into the bright distance making up his wonderful tales. Rose loved his stories any time. For him, it made the heavy hours pass a bit more quickly and took his mind from the thought of Una lying so thin and pale in her darkened room. But he could not shake off his sorrowful mood. Never again would he repeat any of those stories, or write them down for others to read. Only Rose would ever hear them. Now the ragged beggars on the steps filled him with a peculiar fear. He hated their continual pleas, yet he could not be indifferent to them. Suffering, whether his or theirs, weighed him down.

But at home he tried to keep up his cheerful ways. They still played cards every evening, Julian, Rose and their father, who listened always for the tiniest sound from Una's room. He held his cards firmly in a steady hand and played the game with careful attention as if it were the only important thing in the world just at that moment. Even Rose knew, though, how hard he struggled not to show his feelings.

One night his wonderful composure suddenly left him. In the middle of the game he abuptly threw down the cards and rose silently from the table. Rose understood, without words, her father's action. Lately, since they had spent so many hours together daily, Rose often knew her father's thoughts without his telling her of them. A deep understanding had grown up between them.

Later that night as Rose's mother was helping her get ready for bed, Rose suddenly asked:

"Is Una really going to die?"

Her father's troubled eyes had already answered the question for her.

Mrs. Hawthorne looked tenderly at her younger daughter. Until this moment, her heart had been heavy, not only with grief at the thought of losing Una, but with a harsh resentment. It was something her gentle and courageous spirit could not accept. Just now, as she looked at Rose's earnest face, Mrs. Hawthorne felt the bitterness melt away. She smiled quietly and put her arm around Rose.

"Just go to sleep now, and don't worry, dear," she told her.

That night marked the crisis in Una's illness. Next day she began, slowly, to gain strength. There would be many more weeks of rest and constant care, but the danger passed. Una, more serious than ever, seemed a little unwilling to return to life after being so close to death. Although she recovered, she never seemed quite the same. Her thoughts often seemed to carry her away from them and make her almost a stranger to those who loved her most.

Mrs. Hawthorne soon had her cheerful ways again. She seemed to have endless endurance, a way of looking at things that could turn even suffering into joy. Her husband, on the other hand, seemed in times of trouble to be overcome by a sense of foreboding and dread he could not shake off. With a great effort of will he managed to maintain an outward calm, but his heart was often sorrowful. It was almost as if he heard again the echo of a witch's curse spoken centuries before in Salem town.

Spring came again, and gay crowds and flowers were everywhere. Rose and her family were preparing to leave Rome. They would go to England for a while so that Mr. Hawthorne could finish writing his story of the marble faun. Then on to Concord and the Wayside again!

On their last night in Rome they all walked together to the Fountain of Trevi. It was just around the corner from their house and Rose had often lain in bed listening to its musical splashing.

"Whoever throws a coin into Trevi Fountain is sure to return to Rome," her mother had told her.

Now, as she leaned over the stone wall and heard her bright coin splash in the water below, Rose wondered if she too would visit Rome again.

CHAPTER FIVE

Home to Wayside

Coming home to Concord was a terrible disappointment to Rose. After so many years of imagining what Wayside must look like, she had built herself a house very different from the real Wayside.

There it was now, as they drove down the road on a hot June day from the railroad station! A dumpy no-color little place, standing slightly aslant at the foot of the hill. "Nothing

the least bit romantic about it," Rose was telling herself. Memories of Montauto and its old
tower came quickly back.

"How small it's grown," she thought. Surely
this could not be the Wayside of which Una
and Julian, her father and mother too, had
spoken so lovingly all these years. Concord, as
they drove through it, seemed just a very
sleepy one-horse town. And now Rose woke
up suddenly to a rather sad truth. In all her
nine years, she had had no real home and no
real friends.

Here surely was the first of those many disappointments that would punctuate Rose's life.
The great buildup, followed abruptly by the
great letdown! This time it certainly was not
Rose's fault. Most of her years so far had been
spent moving from place to place, meeting famous persons, always being spoiled as the baby
of the family and catered to as the pretty little
daughter of a famous man.

Of course Concord had its famous persons
too. There probably wasn't another town like
it that could boast an Emerson, a Hawthorne,
an Ellery Channing, a Bronson Alcott, a Thoreau. But they were, to a girl of nine, hardly
spectacular in their accomplishments.

In the town's social life, too, Rose found
little to entertain her. The high point of Concord excitement was for the townsfolk to gather
at the Lyceum of an evening to hear one of

the local celebrities lecture. This was dull indeed for a child who had romped in the Vatican gardens and ordered about the guards in
the palace of a Portuguese king.

Mr. Hawthorne in a way shared Rose's feelings in the matter. Homesick abroad, he had
written in his European diary that he needed
the "east winds of Massachusetts" to set his
storyteller's mind in motion once more. Now
he found, strangely, that these very winds blew
a sadness with them and spoke to him in voices
of grief. Why he did not know. Perhaps they
brought overland with them the sea moods that
had wrapped his father and father's father in
shrouds of gloom.

Rose's favorite saying, "When I was in 'Morica," had changed by now to a far more defi-
nite, "When I was in Europe," until even the
four good-natured Alcott girls, who now were
next-door neighbors, grew tired of hearing
about her travels.

"Can't you talk about anything except Italy,
and England and places like that?" demanded
Abby Alcott of Rose one day. At home Mrs.
Alcott was saying the Hawthornes were acting
downright stuck-up now that they had been
abroad.

As for Louisa, Abby's eldest sister, talk of
Europe made her feel more than a little jealous,
though she wouldn't have shown it for the
world. To go abroad was adventurous Louisa's

own private dream, but she had brushed it aside time and again. No, she had made up her mind to stay home where she was really needed. Mr. Alcott, to her a dear, wise and patient father, to others a pioneer in educational ideas, just did not have the knack of earning money. She had seen her mother struggle year after year to carry on bravely under the mounting tide of bills.

"I'll go to work as soon as I can," she had decided. She had kept her word, too, taking all sorts of odd work to earn a few dollars. Of course she kept on writing—stories, plays, poems, practically anything. The Alcotts and the Hawthornes sometimes met in the big old Alcott barn to put on Louisa's wonderful plays. Full of thrilling action, swashbuckling heroes, and fair maidens pining delicately in the background were these dramas, with lifelike costumes whipped up by Louisa herself from odd scraps around the house. She was handy at many things, especially writing. She was in her twenties now, tall, dark-haired and vivacious. The thought had not yet come to her to sit down at that writing table she had in her bare little wing of a room at Apple Slump, as she called their house, and tell the story of the Alcotts themselves. Only then, in the wake of *Little Women*, would fame and fortune come to Louisa.

It was to Abby Alcott that Rose entrusted her own great secret.

"What are you going to be when you grow up?" said Rose to her friend one day as they kept cool under some bushes by the side of the house.

"Why, so far I'm not sure, are you?"

"Yes, I am." Rose's voice had not the shade of uncertainty. "I'm going to be a writer, like Daddy, and make up books."

"Like Louisa?" inquired Abby, who admired her eldest sister very much.

"No, mine are going to be printed and make lots of money. I have a publisher already—Mr. Fields. He does everything Daddy writes, so he'll do mine too." Fancies rose delightfully in Rose's mind, for she remembered her recent trip to Boston with her mother, and the wonderful ices and sweets served to her in such grown-up fashion by the elegant Mrs. Fields.

Inside the house, Mr. Hawthorne sat by the open library window thinking over a scene for the new romance he had started. The voice of Rose, shrill, determined, drifted through the window. "I'm going to be a writer."

Strangely agitated, Mr. Hawthorne called Rose into the house. She knew the moment she saw his face that something was very wrong. He never looked severe, especially to her.

"Don't ever let me hear you talk that way again!" he said sternly. Anger roughened the edge of his voice and flushed his broad brow.

Rose stared at him, puzzled. Why was he, a writer himself, so upset over her choice of a vocation?

"But Daddy—that's what you do."

A sudden impatient motion of his hand stilled her. Her father angry? And at her? She thought of the notebook she had kept hidden for some days now, its pages blackened with slightly smudged writing. The story she had begun had great possibilities except for one thing—spelling. She had learned that to be a writer one must be able to spell, and spelling wasn't Rose's best subject by far!

"If it makes Daddy so angry, writing must be a very exciting life. Yes, maybe even dangerous." His reaction challenged her. She went back to scribbling, more determined than before.

As for Mr. Hawthorne, he didn't like lady writers. Some of them were turning out sentimental stories, worthless from a literary standpoint, but nevertheless very popular. Sometimes they sold fast while the novels of Nathaniel Hawthorne gathered dust on the bookstore shelf.

But there was a much deeper reason why Nathaniel Hawthorne dreaded to think that Rose would turn to serious writing. Sophia would have understood her husband's feeling perfectly, for she had seen him go completely to pieces only once during their life together. That was the night he had finished writing *The*

Scarlet Letter. As always, he sat down to read to her the completed story. As he drew near the end, his strong voice broke and the paper shook in his hand. The great author, whose masterpiece nearly overpowered him, spoke with finality of that occasion in his diary: "Never again will I write anything that stirs me to my very depths as this book did. I could not bear to go through it again."

Far down beneath Mr. Hawthorne's somewhat Puritanical composure lay a hatred for Puritanism itself which he had written out in *The Scarlet Letter* and which he never dared face openly again. It was the shade of Judge Hawthorne who came over and over to threaten him. In *The Scarlet Letter* he had taken up his only weapons, pen and ink and words, to lay low that ghost. But the witch's curse was still ringing in his ears.

As for Rose, she may have sensed her father's hidden fears, though he never spoke of them. His love for his youngest daughter was something special. Una and Julian had come in his youth, in the happy first years of marriage and literary success. Now he felt much older. Rose, separated from him by almost a lifetime, seemed easier to communicate with than the rest. To him she was still a baby, and he continued to write notes calling her baby names.

In the cool dim quiet of the Wayside, Hawthorne was glad to lay away the stiff white cra-
vat and shined-up shoes of his consul days. Instead he put on his old mended sweater and
went out to tie up the beans, hoe potatoes, or
plant a row of corn. Or to walk his favorite
walk, the path up the hill. This at least had not
changed in his absence, though he sensed that
something else was very different. He himself
was not the same.

Again Sophia Hawthorne stepped in to shat-
ter his moodiness with brisk and cheery action.

"Let's build ourselves a tower and have our
own Montauto," she suggested.

The idea was a bit preposterous—an old farmhouse in New England to be taking on the airs
of an Italian villa!

"It would be a wonderful spot for you to
work," went on Mrs. Hawthorne. "High up,
away from all the household clatter." Una and
Julian were older now and would be entertain-
ing their own friends more and more.

What a racket the carpenters made over that
tower while the children played happily amid
the sawhorses, boxes of nails and panes of glass!
After much hammering and sawing, Wayside
had its tower and Mr. Hawthorne could be
alone with his thoughts and the Concord sky.
But writing was becoming harder. Ideas ceased
to come. The old fire was burning down.

Little by little Rose had accepted the people and places of Concord. She was growing very tall.

"She'll be a beauty," the village gossips were saying, "but the way she tosses that red head—independent, that's what she is!"

Lately she had tried more and more to hold her temper in check and to curb her quick tongue. Perhaps she did not quarrel quite so often with Una or with the young Emersons and Alcotts and others who were her companions.

"Did you see her the other night at the masquerade party?" No one could really have failed to see her. Surely she had seemed much more vivid than the other girls. She had gone as Titania, the Fairy Queen. A fanciful notion, no doubt her mother's invention! She wore her full-skirted white dress with an air, and the light danced on its spangles like so many tiny mirrors. There was the crown of silver covered with pearls (make-believe, of course), and the bright green veil made to float out behind her, just so. Mrs. Hawthorne's artistic fingers had worked deftly at the tiny wand tipped with real flowers from the garden. Una undertook to tame the thick red hair into proper curls all around Rose's head.

Then came the blow! Rose, in one of her headlong rushes, fell and sprained her ankle.

She could still go, but the boys couldn't very
well ask her to dance, and perhaps they were
glad, in a way. They were a little hesitant about
even talking to Rose. She could be very distant,
even unfriendly to them at times. Her eyes
seemed to flash a brilliance that was a bit cold
and proud. Perhaps she would be laughing at
them. They didn't know just how to take her.

She had many new interests now. The skating at Walden pond, boating on the river, lawn
parties at Emersons', picnic lunches—she could
enjoy them all with a crowd of friends. She
loved to dress up, and her mother saw to it that
she had many pretty clothes. She loved the re-
freshments at the parties, the nuts and raisins,
cocoanut cakes and lemonade. Then again, she
could be quite bored with them all. Una and
Julian had more grown-up interests, and Rose,
with no great ease in making friends, sometimes felt left out. More than dolls or other
toys she loved her pet kittens. On them she
spent her affection.

Her father was, as always, the center of her
world. Back of the house he had worn a
crooked path among the ferns and berry bushes.
Rose sometimes watched him from the parlor
window as he paced up and down in the dusk.
He was trying to think out his latest novel, *The
Dolliver Romance*. It was coming slowly, slowly
and painfully, and Rose saw with alarm that his
hair was turning whiter day by day.

The question of the freeing of the slaves had become a critical issue. The Abolitionist movement had been gaining ground. All over the country feelings mounted higher and higher, and even in Concord peace was threatened by controversy and dissension. Emerson and his circle put aside long-winded philosophical discussions and waged hot political arguments. Sides were chosen and lifelong friendships broken as the crisis reached its peak.

Mr. Hawthorne had long feared the rift between North and South might lead to violence. The threat of war, ever more real and terrible, cast a pall over him. Then, in April 1861, came the firing on Fort Sumter and the beginning of Civil War.

On the other side of the crooked fence that separated Wayside from the Alcott house, Louisa had come to a decision. She believed strongly in the right of the Negro to his freedom and, characteristically, she was ready to back her opinions with direct action. Watching the young men of the town march off to the battlefront with flags waving and stirring drumbeats, she wished she too could join their ranks. There was, however, one thing she could do. When trouble came to the Alcotts, Louisa was always the strong one. In serious illnesses, she had proved herself a capable nurse. Now she would go to Washington to help nurse the wounded soldiers.

Una Hawthorne went to Alcotts' to help Louisa mark her clothes with indelible ink, and Rose was delighted when her mother sent her over too with a pudding.

In Louisa's low-ceilinged room, Rose sat on the bed and watched Louisa, her dark hair flying, dashing around the room gathering up her things.

"How I wish I could be a nurse too," she exclaimed, "and go with you to take care of wounded soldiers!"

Louisa shook her head violently.

"No, Rose. Let's hope that by the time you're old enough this terrible war will be over—" Then, always sensitive to others' feelings, Louisa saw the crestfallen look on her young friend's face.

"Oh, but then," she hastily went on, "nurses are needed in peace time too, you know. You could be a regular nurse when you grow up."

Rose sat quietly as Louisa finished her packing. She had little realization of what war was, but Louisa's bravery was inspiring. Rose had heard stories of the Underground Railway, the secret network of way stations through which fugitive slaves had been able to escape into free territory. It was even said that the Alcotts had once sheltered a runaway for a night in their big baking oven.

Julian Hawthorne and May Alcott saw Louisa to the Concord station later that December day.

None of them could know, as they waved good-by to their friend, that already the long line of wounded men who would be Louisa's patients had begun to form on Fredericksburg battlefield.

Rose, left behind in outwardly peaceful Concord, often thought of Louisa and the adventures she must be having. Now Rose was ready to give up her dreams of becoming a famous writer. Nursing was much more exciting. Meanwhile, she did her part at home. Aunt Elizabeth Hawthorne, who had come for a visit at Wayside, had taught Rose to knit. Now her bristling needles turned out sock after sock to be sent to the soldiers. Sometimes she studied as she knitted. Mrs. Hawthorne, passing through the room, would pause to look worriedly at her twelve-year-old daughter.

"She's like a harp string, drawn too tight," thought her mother, watching the fierce concentration that brought lines to Rose's young face. With Una, Rose kept busy helping with the housekeeping, sewing, reading. Rose had another assignment too, visiting the ramshackle cottage of an elderly and ailing neighbor to bring baskets of food and try to cheer the old woman. She didn't enjoy these visits. They were tiresome and boring, but Mrs. Hawthorne insisted, so the charitable excursions went on.

Rose also spent many hours practicing on the

piano, but her teacher had no great hopes for
her as a musician. The girl did not lack ambition, nor was she without an artistic appreci-
ation of music, but somehow her fingers on the
keyboard lacked the magical touch that turned
mere notes to lovely sound. Rose was determined to overcome that handicap. Day after
day she sat at the piano, and sometimes she
imagined herself as a brilliant artist thrilling
many listeners with her music.

Louisa's chatty letters home were shared by
the neighborhood. She wrote little of the grim
side of war, of the makeshift ill-equipped hospital, of the days and nights without sleep, of
her homesickness. She told instead of the soldiers she talked to, their stories of home and
family, and especially about the little drummer,
twelve years old, who had valiantly marched to
battle with his regiment and later had been
gently carried back to Louisa's warmhearted
care.

One day, about six weeks after Louisa's departure, the Alcotts received an urgent message
from Washington. Louisa was very ill. Mr.
Alcott, forgetting for a time the ideal world
he was always trying to fashion, rushed down
to bring his daughter home. She had not wanted
to give up, even though terribly sick, but now
she hardly noticed as her father carried her to
the train in the capital city, and then, much
later, into her familiar room in Concord. For

many weeks she was dangerously ill, and when she at last got up, all her wonderful drive and energy were gone. By that time Rose and the others had learned to tiptoe to the Alcott door to inquire for their friend in whispers. In April, Louisa could venture out again to sit under the big tree, but her health had been badly affected. Once Rose saw her crying, pale and tortured by some memories of the war.

For several months, Mr. Hawthorne had written nothing. Each day he locked himself in his tower retreat and tried to go on with his writing. Each day the blank sheets of paper lay maddeningly before him, his pen slack in his fingers and his mind wandering far from the story he wanted to put down. It was to him as though the war were a personal sorrow. This time even the tireless sunniness of Sophia could not help him.

She said nothing as she watched his strikingly handsome face grow thin and tired. He still smiled, but with a visible effort. Rose, too, keenly sensed the change in her father. His eyes as he looked at her were strange and sad.

"You look all pearl and rose," he said, admiring her new party dress. She was a tall girl now, and her white muslin dress with its short ruffled sleeves and blue sash became her very well. But when he repeated his old jokes and little comedies Rose no longer felt like laughing.

One day she stood at the parlor window watching him go up his old path toward the grove of trees. There were huckleberry bushes beside it, and pale purple violets underfoot, among the dry brown leaves. This time she shivered coldly as she looked, for his shoulders were bent and he seemed almost a stranger.

Julian was away at college then, but those at home did their best to pretend all was well. It was as if each one were hiding his own knowledge out of love for the rest. Mr. Hawthorne himself took part in this deception that deceived no one, but in one of his letters to his publisher about his book he seemed to speak with sad but unresentful clarity.

"I shall never finish it. . . . Say to the public what you think best. . . . I am not low-spirited, nor fanciful, nor freakish, but look what seem to be realities in the face, and am ready to take whatever may come."

But he was careful to hide this from those he loved most. He did not want to consult a doctor, but his old friend, Dr. Oliver Wendell Holmes, had seen him and felt he suffered from a mysterious illness no drug of his could relieve.

Once again, as during Una's Roman illness, Franklin Pierce came to his friend's aid.

"Perhaps," he suggested sympathetically to Mrs. Hawthorne, "a little trip might do him good. It would cheer him up and take his mind off himself."

"He always did like traveling," replied Mrs. Hawthorne gratefully. She was ready to try any remedy.

"We could take an easy tour up through New Hampshire. He likes the scenery there. We'll go by short stages, in an open carriage, so he can be in the air."

Mr. Hawthorne accepted the invitation politely and made ready to go. Rose stood at the gate as he left to meet Mr. Pierce in Boston. He stood straight as always, but the strain of it told in his face. He smiled at Rose and bade her good-by with kind tenderness.

Mrs. Hawthorne's heart was heavy, but she tried to act cheerful. Rose's birthday was coming, her thirteenth, and she must have a party as always.

There were games, Rose's favorite cakes, and friends to share the fun. It was May, with beautiful weather and all the world about Wayside breaking into leaf and bloom. Up on the hill-path the ferns unfurled their lacy fronds.

When the party was over, a messenger rode up to the gate. Nathaniel Hawthorne, he told them, had died quietly while sleeping in a hotel room in Plymouth, New Hampshire, where he and Mr. Pierce had stopped for the night.

Rose looked down at the white party dress she had thought so pretty. All its ribbons and

ruffles seemed ridiculously silly. Through her
tears she looked up the little crooked path and
saw that it was indeed empty and the tall dear
figure would not walk there again.

CHAPTER SIX

Romantic Dresden

Rose tossed her head and her gray eyes snapped.

"Oh Mother," she said crossly, "I don't want to go. Swimming parties bore me, and besides—"

"But Rose," her mother interrupted gently, "you know the Emersons are giving this party especially for you!"

"Can't you understand?" Rose insisted. "I just don't want to go. I hate parties."

Mrs. Hawthorne shook her head silently and went back downstairs to her sewing. She sat down and took up a dress of Rose's. She would finish the hem before dinner. Rose herself had begun letting it down, but with her usual impatience had given up the job when it was half done.

The girls did all their own sewing now, with Mrs. Hawthorne's help, for they had not been able to afford the dressmaker. Una and Rose had really been wonderful about it all, their mother thought now, as her needle skipped along in tiny even stitches. They had willingly, even gaily, shared the work of keeping the Wayside in order, for now they had no maid. Rose had even taken up painting little souvenirs to be sold in one of the village stores.

Yes, they had all done their best to keep life at the Wayside, outwardly at least, just what it had been in happier years. Yet, though the girls looked pretty in their homemade clothes, and the house was as fragrant as ever with fresh-cut garden flowers, and though their friend Franklin Pierce had very generously offered to pay Julian's tuition at Harvard that year, Sophia Hawthorne sometimes felt even her brave spirit weighed down with worry. They had so little money coming in from the sale of her husband's novels. Besides, the children were older now and there were so many important decisions about their future that she must make alone.

Just now it was Rose who worried her. At times the girl was very puzzling. Today she did not want to go swimming with the rest of the crowd at Walden Pond. Yet, other days, she would come home bubbling with excitement over an outing—a boat trip with Una and some college boys or a picnic in the woods.

Mrs. Hawthorne reached the end of her hem and held up the dress, shaking it briskly to see if it would hang straight. It was a nice dress, even if it were last year's, she thought, and with the new trimming Rose had put on it would look very well.

"She really needs a new hat," thought Sophia. "I wish I could get her one. Maybe just this one time I could squeeze five dollars." For the hundredth time she mentally added up the bills —the coal, the groceries, Julian's allowance—and the next royalty check from the publishing house in Boston was not due for some time!

Upstairs in her room Rose's mind was not on hats, dresses, or even the swimming party she did not feel like attending. She was wishing she had someone really sympathetic to talk to. Of course Una was always understanding, but she was so grown up now. Besides, Una was in love, and that made her even dreamier than usual. At times she hardly seemed to hear what Rose was saying to her.

As for her mother, Rose had learned that her

own very direct way of speaking often left her gentle sentimental mother a little breathless.

No, the best way for Rose to tell her troubles was on paper. She had found lately that she could express her thoughts in letters much better than when talking. Her Aunt Elizabeth already had a sizeable pile of letters from this impetuous young niece whose moods often troubled those around her.

"I feel responsible for my life," Rose had told her once. Yet at times the future looked bleak to her for she felt she had no great talents. "For though I know what is good, and love God, yet I am very good-for-nothing," she had explained.

Perhaps it was quite natural for the child of such gifted parents to be discouraged at times, for Rose had learned from Nathaniel and Sophia Hawthorne that artistic achievements bring life's greatest rewards. If this was a rather one-sided view, the Hawthornes themselves could not be blamed. In the New England of their time, just emerging from colonial and Puritan ways of thinking, there was a great deal of emphasis on cultural development.

"Just because heaven does not choose that I should be a genius, I am miserable. . . . I shall never have the rare pleasure of being loved infinitely." Rose could not find her ideal in any of the boys she knew. She still did not feel at ease with them. Nor did they know quite how to take her, for her manner was cool and distant, and she did not seem to be at all interested in what they said or did.

Until she was thirteen Rose had never attended regular school. Since then she had spent short periods, none too happy, at about four different schools. She had not found them easy. Making friends was hard for her. Then too, her early years of travel had not given her the basic knowledge she needed for higher studies. Even now, her letters showed many words spelled oddly in her own original way.

The school she had liked best was the one run in Lexington by Mr. Dio Lewis whose educational ideas were thought very new and different. Gymnastic exercises and a healthy outdoor life were part of his plan. Here, in the casual sport clothes and relaxed atmosphere Mr. Lewis advocated, Rose had felt for a time much happier. Then fire destroyed the school.

Rose had worked very hard at her studies. "I have neither beauty nor fascination to attract my friends," she had explained in one of her letters, "but I hope I shall be able to sing, make music, draw and paint. . . . I wish to read a great deal, to be learned. I have great ambitions."

She was able to carry out at least one of them right away. She read all of her father's books, seeing in them this time many things she had not seen before. She felt very close to her father through his work. His way of writing brought back the way he had looked and even his tone of voice in speaking to her.

"It is," she told someone, "as if he were to speak to me, and I were to see his face!" When Mrs. Hawthorne sat with the girls in the garden at Wayside and read again the story they had heard him tell so often of the Miraculous Pitcher, Rose felt that her father was talking directly to her.

About this time Mrs. Hawthorne came to a decision. Why shouldn't they all go to Europe and live for a while? Concord did not seem to be the ideal place for them just then. Una's romance had ended unhappily, Julian was restless with his Harvard studies, and Rose was having more ups and downs than usual.

"Let's rent the Wayside for now and move to Dresden," she suggested one evening when they were all together around the big dining table.

"Why Dresden, Mother?" Julian wanted to know.

"For one thing, Julian, you could study at the Realschule there. It's one of the best engineering schools in the world," she replied.

Rose looked up from her plate. It was easy to see the idea pleased her.

"How I'd love to get away from this town!" she exclaimed, and then added more thoughtfully, "and Dresden, I know, is famous for its art schools. Maybe I could take up painting in earnest there."

"Just what I was thinking, Rose," her mother agreed, pleased that her suggestion had met with the enthusiasm of her younger daughter.

Una sat at the other side of the table trying hard to seem hungry, though she wasn't at all.

"Maybe a trip would be a good thing just now, Mother," she agreed quietly. Tonight her eyes were dreamy and faraway. Other times they would flash with feelings strangely violent. Una was a mysterious person.

Sophia Hawthorne did not tell her children the main reason for the move. Dresden was an inexpensive place to live and she had to be careful with her limited income.

Once again the traveling Hawthornes packed up and set off across the ocean. Seventeen-year-old Rose had no regrets as she left Concord town far behind. She had never liked it much anyhow.

Dresden, they soon found, was a pleasant and picturesque place. It lay on both sides of the River Elbe and had many bridges, old and new, crossing and recrossing the water dividing it. Long ago, as capital of Saxony, Dresden had been a city of palaces and towers. Since then, its famous art treasures had drawn many visitors from other lands.

Mrs. Hawthorne, with Una and Julian, set-

tled down at a pleasant boarding house where
other students were also living. Rose stayed for
a while at a school nearby. By this time she was
painfully learning that getting along with people
was not her special gift. Here the situation was
not made any easier by the fact that she was a
foreigner, and a privileged one at that. She
was allowed to leave the school several times a
week for art lessons. And on chilly nights she
could have a fire in her room. It could not help
arousing the antagonism of the other girls. Rose,
sailing past them with head held high and no
smile on her face, did very little to make
friends.

"No one," she wrote to her Aunt Mary
Mann back in New England, "can tell how
often and severe my struggles are to be good,
any more than they could ever believe how sincere and great my hope is that I shall sometime
overcome myself, and be charitable, humble,
and altogether righteous."

Rose might explain her troubles at length in
letters to her American relatives, but she did
not welcome sympathy from those around her.
Even when Julian good-naturedly tried to pry
into her thoughts, in a bantering way, Rose
would often feel her temper rising and sharp
words on her tongue.

Several times Julian took Rose to dances and
parties and introduced her to his friends, hoping
that she would make some of her own. Each

time it was disappointing. Julian, who made friends very easily, could not understand his sister's apparent coldness toward the young men she met. At first they were attracted by her beauty, but when they tried to talk to her she would stare down at the floor and act as if she did not welcome their friendship.

"I am notable for getting on the wrong side of people," she admitted.

Poor Rose! She took things very seriously and, like so many of us, was sharply disappointed whenever her actions fell short of her ideals.

Mrs. Hawthorne, however, always had the greatest hopes for her son and daughters and rarely saw any faults in them. She was very happy over their new life. Once an enthusiastic tourist and tireless sight-seer, Sophia was now satisfied with a quieter existence. Much of her time was spent working on her writing.

For many years Nathaniel Hawthorne had kept journals and diaries of his day-to-day experiences and thoughts. Now the public wanted to read them. Mrs. Hawthorne could not allow them to be published until she had gone over each page carefully. She wanted to be sure there was nothing that might cast any doubts upon her husband's nobility of character. Word for word she was editing these journals, blotting out phrases and sentences here and there where a too personal reference to herself or some other member of the family had appeared, or where her husband's occasionally strong expressions seemed to destroy the poetic quality of his style.

This is what she was working on day after day upstairs in her cosy room. Some of the old bustling energy had left her now, but her graying hair seemed only to add dignity to her pretty face and lively eyes.

Downstairs, at the dinner table, there was always interesting talk with the other students. Mrs. Hawthorne had learned German years ago, but the girls found it hard to follow the conversation.

Although the city of Dresden had a gay and sociable spirit, Rose found little time at first for fun. She was working very hard on her art. She studied and painted furiously. Mrs. Hawthorne had felt for some time that Rose had a great talent, and now, in a city of many art masterpieces, Rose too was seized by the dream of becoming a famous painter. For hours she stood in the galleries of the Grosse Garten, Dresden's huge public park, studying its greatest treasure, the Madonna of Raphael.

Julian meanwhile had lost no time in making friends. One day he brought two schoolmates to meet his sisters. "This is Francis Lathrop," he announced, glancing at the taller of the boys, "and his brother George."

The Lathrops too had come to Dresden to

study. Their mother was with them, and their father was serving as United States consul in Honolulu.

"George and Francis can help you learn German if anyone can," Julian told Una and Rose half-seriously. "At least, they've taught me a good deal."

George spoke up quickly with a flashing smile. "It would be an honor to have two such fair pupils," he said, with a courtly bow. His dark eyes took in Una's stately beauty and Rose's more dramatic good looks. George Lathrop at seventeen was supremely sure of himself.

"I doubt if I can ever learn this language," Una said. "The words are so hard to pronounce."

"Oh, don't worry. We'll start right now," said George enthusiastically. "Let's hear you say 'Mohrenkopfe.'"

"All right. 'Moh-ren-kopfe'—but what a terrible sounding word! What can it mean?" Una looked at the younger Lathrop questioningly. She seemed as delicate and fragile as the Meissen porcelain figurines for which Dresden was so famous.

"Don't you know? Why, it means the most delicious, most wonderful chocolate-covered cream puffs in the world. And Francis and I know just where to find them. A little café not too far from here. How about it—shall we all go right now?"

That was the beginning of many good times for the five friends. Francis Lathrop was a very gifted artist. As for George, he planned to make writing his career. Already he had had several pieces published. George had not only a talent for writing. He had boundless confidence in his own powers and looked forward to a successful future. He always seemed to have the right word for every situation while the quieter Francis lacked his younger brother's air of bravado.

Together they visited the city's picturesque places, spent hours talking in dimly lit cafés, and listened to music played outdoors in the Grosse Garten. One day Francis announced important news.

"I've been invited to go to London and study with the great Whistler," he told the others, his usually quiet voice excited.

"How wonderful!" Una exclaimed. "But how soon are you leaving?"

"In about a week," Francis said, and then added, "in a way, I shall miss Dresden, but this is too big an opportunity to miss." He looked at the two Hawthorne sisters with whom he had enjoyed so many good times.

"Tell you what!" George jumped up from his chair, his dark eyes bright with a new idea. "Let's all celebrate. We have a few days left together. What do you say? We'll go to all the places we've liked the best."

It was spring in Dresden, and after the cold gray months of winter the old city seemed unbelievably lovely. Soon the day came for Francis and George to leave and the friends parted a little sadly.

Mrs. Hawthorne, now working on a book of her own memoirs, decided not long afterward that she too would prefer London. She was not feeling well these days, and perhaps the change would do her good.

Una went to England with her mother. Julian had given up his engineering studies and gone back to America to take a job. Rose wanted to stay on in Dresden. She had taken up music too, and now divided her day between the piano and the easel. But her hopes of great success were growing small.

"It is wonderful how little I have managed to learn in these twelve months," she wrote in a letter in November 1869. "The piano is somewhat of a trial to me. . . . I practice till the tips of my two little fingers wear off, and make a terrible hullabaloo."

The art lessons were somewhat better, yet even a kind teacher like Herr Wagner could not hold out truthfully any great promise for Rose's future as a painter.

Left alone in a city whose soul seemed to

be art and music, Rose at times felt very discouraged.

"Can there be anything in me worth pro-
ducing?" she wrote one day. "If so, it will be
something far higher than my best self that
works through my hand." Certainly she had
some purpose in life, some special calling. Her
belief in God told her so. At times she had
even felt her faith was deserting her, but these
trials now had passed.

She planned to live permanently in Europe,
traveling through the beautiful Rhine valley,
spending part of each year at Rome. Then
history stepped in to change all that. With the
outbreak of the Franco-Prussian War, she had
to leave Dresden quickly and join her mother
and Una in their little London apartment.

The two sisters roamed around the London
they had known as children, taking in many
things they had missed before. One day they
found themselves in a very poor section, a
street of tumble-down houses and ragged boys
and girls.

Suddenly Una stood still. Her usually peaceful face took on a look of intense feeling.

"Look at them, Rose," she said. "These poor
little ones have no one to look after them. I
wish that I could help them!"

Rose glanced briefly along the littered street.
"Oh, come on, Una. Don't even look at that

ugly scene!" She took her sister's arm firmly and would have started off toward home.

"No, wait, Rose." Una's eyes burned with a mysterious fire. "Don't you remember? These are the very people Dad wrote about in his book about England. He saw them too, and he felt just as I do about them."

"Of course, anybody would feel sorry for them. But they can't really be helped. They're used to living like this. Don't forget, Dad didn't like to be near such people, even if he did feel sorry for them. And I'm the same way."

This time Rose succeeded in pulling Una toward the opposite corner.

"All right, Rose," said the older girl as she turned to go, "but some day maybe you'll feel differently. Maybe you'll feel, as I do, that there is a lot to be done, and that you yourself can do it!"

It did not take the Lathrops long to learn that their Dresden friends were also in London. They came for a visit, bringing as a gift two lovely scarves Francis had painted.

George, as usual, was handsome, swaggering and full of good spirits. He told of his success in writing for an American newspaper.

"And I'm learning to make stained glass windows," said Francis. The evening passed quickly, and Rose felt that George's dark eyes

were often on her. She was glad that she had
worn her prettiest dress.

"But it's really Una that George likes,"
Rose told herself afterward. That was how it
had seemed in Dresden.

Next morning a letter came for Rose addressed in George's unmistakably bold hand-
writing. Inside, without signature or explanation, was a poem. Rose read it quickly. Then
she read it again. A romantic gesture, or an
expression of deep feeling? She did not know,
but she was sure of one thing. It was she,
and not Una, in whom George was interested.

They began to meet often then. George was
working as a correspondent for the *New York
Independent*. Rose had never felt very sure of
herself, but George had confidence to spare. If
she felt awkward and silent in company, his
bright talk and funny stories put everyone at
ease.

For some time Mrs. Hawthorne had tried to
hide from her daughters the fact that she was
far from well. Now she could keep the secret
no longer. She had met every challenge of life
with cheerful courage, but this was the hardest
test of all. Una and Rose watched many days
by her bedside as the winter dragged endlessly
on. Just as the first spring flowers began to
open, Mrs. Hawthorne's brave battle came to
an end. The tiny golden flower Rose laid on
the coverlet seemed to symbolize her mother's

life. Sophia Hawthorne had looked confidently for beauty everywhere, and almost always found it.

Now Rose and Una, finding themselves very much alone, were thankful that they had such good friends as the Lathrops to help them over the lonely time that followed. Julian was married and had his own family in New York. The Wayside had been sold during their European stay.

Julian wrote and offered them a home with him.

"I'll go back to New York with you," George offered generously, for it was not the custom then for young ladies to cross the ocean alone. "Don't worry about anything. I'll take care of all the details."

In their room in Shaftesbury Street, Rose and Una sat sadly among their cluttered belongings and the half-packed suitcases.

"What shall we do when we get to New York?" Rose was asking unhappily. "Julian can't support us and his own family too."

Una stood up and walked over to the window. She looked out thoughtfully for a moment before turning back to Rose.

"I must tell you something, Rose—" she began hesitantly. "I've—I've decided not to go back to America."

"Not going back? But you'll be here all

alone—" Rose paused abruptly as the answer to her unasked question dawned upon her.

Una's face was paler than usual. She had been through a severe strain during their mother's illness, but the mysterious fire burned even brighter in her eyes.

"Remember that day we walked—those children we saw? Well, it's for them I am staying. I want to do something for them."

"Are you sure that's what you want, Una?" Rose asked.

"More than anything else in the world," Una replied firmly. She turned to her younger sister. "And you, Rose—what do you want?"

Rose did not reply right away. Una put an arm gently around Rose's shoulders.

"Is it George?" she asked.

For once Rose did not pull away with an impatient gesture.

"He's asked me to marry him," she said quietly.

"And what did you tell him?"

"I haven't, yet. But I think the answer will be 'yes.'"

CHAPTER SEVEN

"Sorrow, My Friend"

Rose and George were married that September in London. She was not yet twenty-one. When the midnight bells rang to welcome in the New Year of 1872, the young Lathrops were on the high seas coming home to America. Life looked bright and full of hope.

They both intended to write. Between them they would make a good living.

One day George came back to their New

York apartment with a small paper parcel in his hand and a special twinkle in his dark eyes.

"For you, Rösl," he announced gaily. "A little surprise!"

She tore off the wrapping. It was a book of George's poems, dedicated to her. She read the title, *Rose and Roof Tree*. How typical it was of George's generous and gallant ways to do this for her!

When he was offered an editorial job on the *Atlantic Monthly* magazine, he accepted eagerly. They moved to Boston. Now they would have a regular income, something a bit more dependable than occasional checks from an article or story sold. "Now we can really settle down, Rösl," George told her. "We'll have a nice home and all the bills will be paid on time."

Rose tried hard to get used to housekeeping. She did not like to admit to herself that sweeping, dusting and cooking really did not interest her very much. All too often, in the middle of the morning, she would stop, dustcloth in hand, to sit at her desk and scribble down a story that had come to her mind. Quickly she would fill several sheets of paper with the outline of an idea. Then, just as suddenly, she would put it aside and go on to doing something else.

"Why don't you finish this up?" George would ask, after glancing over some of these hasty jottings. "I think you have the makings of a good story here."

"Oh, I don't know," Rose would answer absently. "I'm tired of that idea now. Maybe I'll think of a better one."

George did not work this way at all. He too had many ideas, but he had learned that to produce a finished work he must stick to one idea through many rewritings.

"You know, dear, ideas aren't hard to find. It's the writing that's work. All good writers have to put in many hours of tiresome effort before their stories can appear in finished form."

George's criticisms, gentle as they were, hurt Rose deeply. Perhaps at heart she suspected he was right, but pride kept her from accepting his wise advice. Hadn't her father, after all, been America's leading novelist?

Still, the hard work of writing discouraged her, and though some editors, doubtless in respect to her father's memory, published an occasional story she sent them, she was less successful than George. He kept turning out articles, stories, and even books with amazing speed.

Much of Rose's life had been spent moving from place to place. Now she found it hard to settle down and feel at home. Perhaps the good Sophia Hawthorne, too anxious to develop the cultural side of her daughter's nature, had

made Rose more at ease in an art gallery than
in her own kitchen.

The Lathrops moved several times. Rose did
not have her mother's knack for fixing things
in a homey and attractive way, nor did she
have Mrs. Hawthorne's gift of thrifty manage-
ment. Sometimes they even had to borrow
money when the bills mounted too high.

Una came from England for a visit. She told
Rose and George of her work, as a member
of an Anglican social service organization, with
the poor children of London.

"But Una," Rose said, "I still don't understand how you can go into those awful houses
—so dirty—why, it's actually dangerous, I'm
sure."

"If you could see those little faces," replied
Una, "just waiting for any kindness, any love—
you wouldn't say that."

"Perhaps it's the right work for you," Rose
admitted after a while, "but I could never do
it!"

"Rose, don't you remember the day we
walked together down that street in London
and you told me the same thing? I reminded
you then, and I want to tell you again now—
read what Dad wrote about his visit to the
slums in *Our Old Home*."

Rose nodded politely. "I'll read it some day,"

she told her sister. "But now let's have coffee, shall we?"

Rose hurried away, the folds of her pale gold silk dress falling softly as she moved.

"How beautiful she looks!" thought Una, gazing after her. "But I wonder if she is truly happy."

In the kitchen, Rose thoughtfully filled the coffee pot with water. There was a sort of radiance about Una, she thought, a light coming from within, even though she was thinner and paler than ever. A feeling something like disappointment, or perhaps even akin to envy, came over Rose, but she tried to push it away. Could it be that Una had found in a life of self-sacrifice a happiness greater than hers?

Firmly she put such thoughts out of her mind as she laid out on a tray her prettiest cups and saucers and prepared a plate of tiny cakes.

When Una had returned to England and her settlement work, Rose thought often of the spirit of dedication that had glowed like a flame through her sister's fragile frame. The mystery of Una's vocation puzzled her, yet she was not ready to seek its explanation in her father's writings as Una had urged her to do.

While visiting America, Una had fallen in love with a young man and they had planned to be married. But it seemed that Una was not destined for ordinary happiness. The young

man's health failed suddenly and he died before they could meet again. Una accepted the
tragic news very calmly, almost as if she had
known the marriage would never take place.
She was willing to accept sacrifice as the central fact of her life, but those near her noticed
her lovely tawny hair had turned to gray very
quickly.

She had joined the Anglican Church and had
gone to stay near an Anglican convent in
Windsor. Perhaps she hoped to become a nun
there eventually, but hard work and disappointment had weakened too much her already frail
body. A sudden illness overtook her, and almost before the news of it could reach
America, another letter had to be sent telling
Rose that Una had died. It had all happened
so quickly that Rose was stunned. Yet she
could not say that Una had not lived a full
and complete and very satisfying life, even in
so few years.

In a way it seemed as if Una had carried
on the tradition of the doomed Hawthornes of
Salem. Her father in many a dark moment
had feared greatly for this child of his, more
delicate and sensitive than the others. Could it
be that she had inherited the mysterious family
curse? Even to those who loved her best, Una
Hawthorne had been a shadowy spirit, lovely,
dreamlike, yet capable of intense dedication
and tireless work for the poor she loved.

In Boston a wonderful new happiness had come to Rose with the birth of a son, a little boy with gray-blue eyes and red hair like his mother.

"George," Rose said one day as they stood over the baby's crib and watched him sleeping, his tiny hands tightly curled on top of the blanket, "I wish we could have him baptized."

George looked at his wife with surprise. Her request startled him, for after all, Rose had never been a churchgoer. Her religious views were seldom expressed in any outward act of devotion.

"Of course, dear, if you want it," he agreed after a moment.

They took him to the nearest church and had him baptized Francis, after his uncle Francis Lathrop.

Now the days seemed to rush by quickly. Rose did not have much time to sit at her desk and scribble stories, for Francie soon began to run about. He had to be watched carefully in the small apartment and taken out for daily airings.

She proposed another startling idea to George one evening after dinner.

"Couldn't we buy Wayside again?" she asked.

George put down the manuscript he was reading.

"Well, I don't know," he answered. "Maybe

we could manage it. But I thought you didn't like it. You told me you never wanted to live there."

"I did feel that way," explained Rose, "but now Francie needs room to run and play. Wayside would be wonderful for him. He could be out on the lawn all day."

George was always enthusiastic about anything that brought Rose happiness. They arranged to leave Boston and go back to the little old house on Lexington Road. There Rose, with her new family, settled down among old memories, the things she had grown up with, even the threadbare chair where her father had sat telling stories of the Miraculous Pitcher or of Jason and the Golden Fleece.

Now, if ever, Rose could be happy. It was comforting to her to see around her all the shabby familiar things of her own childhood. Francie grew sturdy and brown, roaming the same woodland paths, lying on the smooth pine needles on the hill.

When Francie was five years old, George came home from work one afternoon to find Rose hurrying anxiously down the walk to meet him.

"Francie's sick," she told him. George saw the worry in her eyes and tenderly tried to ease it away.

They went upstairs. George put his hand on

the boy's forehead. It felt too warm. Francie
opened his eyes slowly. His voice sounded dull.
Weakly he put his arms up to his father.

"Lift me up, Daddy," he whispered faintly,
"way up in the sky." It was a little game they
had each night after George came home.

Tonight the father tried to hide his concern.
"Oh, children often have things like this," he
told Rose consolingly. "High fevers and all
that! They come and go quickly."

But Francie's fever did not go. The doctor
was discouraging. Rose watched beside the little
boy, but after a short few days, as he lay
very quiet in the darkened room, she knew
that another dream of happiness had been shat-
tered. Never again would George lift his son
high up in his strong arms. Instead, with tears
in his eyes, he wrote a sad poem that ended:

"Another Father now, more strong than I,
  Has borne you voiceless to your dear blue
  sky."

Now indeed Rose could bear the Wayside
no more. For the second time it was too full
of sad memories. The house was sold to a Mrs.
Lothrop, an author of books too, whose stories
of the Five Little Peppers were being read by
young people everywhere.

Once again Rose packed her well-worn suitcases. This time she and George would try to forget their grief in a trip to England and Spain.

In New York's Greenwich Village, the lights burned brilliantly at 55 Clinton Place. Everything was in readiness for a party, and already a few glittering and famous personalities had begun to gather. Mrs. Gilder, the hostess, sat quietly by the big fireplace, her knitting in her lap. Her guests were quite used to finding her this way, week after week, for her Friday night "at-homes" were famous gatherings. Besides, it was really Mr. Gilder who kept the party going at a lively pace. Richard Watson Gilder was not only editor of the important *Century* magazine, but a leading poet and critic. Around him circulated a group that included many of the most talented writers and artists of the day.

Mrs. Gilder rose from her chair to see if the chocolate and biscuits were ready to serve. A tall dark-haired young woman came across the now-crowded room to speak to her.

"Who is that new couple over there? I don't remember seeing them here before."

Mrs. Gilder answered in a low voice, "Oh, the Lathrops—George and Rose. They're living in New York now. She's the daughter of Hawthorne, you know."

"Really? How interesting! And how gorgeous she looks with that flaming red hair!"

"Come on over," said Mrs. Gilder, taking her guest by the arm. "I'll introduce you."

Rose was sitting quietly listening as George entertained a small group around them with one of his witty stories.

"This is Emma Lazarus," said Mrs. Gilder. Rose turned her head and found herself looking into a pair of unusually large and beautiful eyes. The face of Emma Lazarus showed quite clearly what sort of person she was, gentle, compassionate, highly intelligent. Rose, who made friends very slowly and had often felt quite lost in the gay company of the Gilders' acquaintances, immediately felt at ease. They began to talk, Rose forgetting altogether the rather aloof dignity which sometimes made people think her a bit unsociable.

It was the beginning of a real friendship. Rose learned that behind the burning eyes of this Jewish girl burned an equally fiery ambition. The daughter of a well known and wealthy merchant, Emma might have enjoyed a life of ease and social position. But the tragedy of the Jewish people, at that time suffering cruel persecution in Russia, troubled her deeply. She longed to help them through writing of their plight.

When the Statue of Liberty was unveiled in New York harbor on a misty gray October

day in 1886, it was the words of Emma Lazarus that were engraved upon its base.

"Send them, the tempest-tossed, to me.

I lift my lamp beside the golden door."

She had not written *The New Colossus* with
its moving lines merely as empty inscriptions for
a piece of statuary. She had expressed her own
sympathy for exiles and her longing to find
them a refuge.

Rose admired greatly the self-sacrificing spirit
of her friend. Perhaps Emma reminded her of
Una, who in her own way had lived that
dedication to an ideal. Wistfully, and with sadness, Rose had begun to wish she herself could
do something to help others. Childless now, not
too successful as a writer, she found herself
drifting without any consuming interest in anything.

Besides, another disappointing fact grew clearer
to her day by day. Since Francie's death, things
had not gone too well between Rose and
George. They had always had quarrels, the
sharp disagreements common to persons of strong
will, quick temper, and impetuous acts.

Friends began to notice Rose's letters came
from many different addresses as the ever-mov-
ing Lathrops went from hotel room to apartment to furnished room and back to hotel again.
Sometimes, feeling the need to be alone after
an especially bitter quarrel, Rose would go off
and rent a room by herself. Soon George,

truly sorry for his part in the trouble and full of gallant promises to do better in the future, would persuade her that all was well again between them.

Strangely enough, George's very sociable nature—one of the qualities that had so attracted Rose to him—was causing one of the most serious problems. At his frequent gatherings with writers and other friends, there was always a certain amount of drinking. Almost without noticing it, George had begun taking more and more, till now he sometimes lost count of the number of times his glass was refilled in an evening.

It was good to be able to forget for a time that he and Rose disagreed more and more often, that after years of marriage they still lived as transients without a real home, and that they had lost their only child. More than that, there was a haunting doubt in him as the success he had always expected so confidently was long in coming. His writings were good. They were praised and admired. His talents were equally impressive in prose and poetry. Yet somehow he had just missed being a great writer, and to be merely a very good one hurt him perhaps more than outright failure would have done.

The tragedy of not being a literary genius would have been enough, but to be married to the daughter of Nathaniel Hawthorne and not

be a literary genius was too much for George.
Sometimes this made him resent Rose herself, as
if she were a constant reminder of a painful
comparison.

So, as the dream of greatness faded farther
and farther into the distance, George tried to
forget his disillusion in drink. It was a habit that
grew steadily worse, and one that he never
seemed able to overcome.

Again and again he resolved to do better. And
Rose resolved to be more patient and to help
him along. They were always making new
starts. One of these consisted in moving to a
pretty house in New London, Connecticut.
Here Rose put forth a sincere effort at home-
making, even to painting one of the floors
pink! Not everyone who saw it approved of it,
though by now Rose's friends knew that she
was always doing surprising things.

Even so, they were shocked when even
stranger news went around. The Lathrops had
become Catholics! Few had suspected that Rose
and George had even a passing interest in religion. But then, independent Mrs. Lathrop seldom explained her reasons to anyone! In this
case at least she was wise, too wise to try to
account for the gift of faith.

In New London they had found close friends
in Alfred and Adelaide Chappell. Mr. Chappell
had planned to be an Episcopalian minister, but
had given this up and later become a Catholic.

In Boston, George and Rose had made the acquaintance of the dynamic John Boyle O'Reilly, editor of the Boston *Pilot*. The story of his famous escape by sea from the British penal colony to which he had been sent for taking part in the Irish nationalist movement was not his only distinction. He was also a noted poet, editor, and tireless crusader for justice.

All these persons, and others, in their immediate circle certainly had something to do with the Lathrops' decision to become Catholics.

As far as Rose was concerned, there were other influences, some deeply buried in her memory, half-forgotten yet powerful. The Roman days of her childhood, when she had felt the warmth of glowing faith in ancient churches; the moment when the hand of the Holy Father, Pius IX, had rested gently on her tumbled curls; the shadow of the maid-servant Stella, kneeling before her big crucifix in the cavernous twilight rooms of Montauto; the tiny wax Bambino sleeping forever in His glass crêche; the hidden simple devotion of the plain Catholic people she had met and known throughout her life. Yes, and the marble statue of Rose of Lima, first saint canonized from the Americas, in the Staffa Palace!

Even before these, there had been the sad mysterious look in the eyes of Nathaniel Hawthorne, the long black shade of Judge Hawthorne's Puritan hat and cape, the beseeching

eyes of a condemned woman of Salem, and her
father's unfinished pilgrimage toward a religious
faith.

Whether she could have or would have explained it, all these had a part in bringing Rose
to kneel before Father Alfred Young of the
Paulist Fathers and profess her faith.

If Rose had hoped that religious conversion
would straighten the stormy course of her marriage, she was disappointed, and bitterly so.

George's valiant struggle to control his drinking had not succeeded.

"This time—this time I'll make good. I
promise I will." He had promised sincerely over
and over. But his "one more chance" had
stretched into tiresome and ever more trying
repetitions.

"And I—I'll try to be more patient. I'll keep
my temper," Rose had resolved.

"I love you, Rose. I'll do it this time, for
you!" George had some of his old swagger still,
and much of his youthful charm, but very little
of his self-confidence!

Hearing his well-meant but empty promise,
Rose one day knew for certain that it was all
over, humanly speaking, between them. By
1895 they sadly agreed that they could not get
along together. Church authorities gave them
permission to separate. Rose, after more than
twenty years of marriage, found herself again

with all her hopes broken around her. She was no longer an idealistic young girl. Only a short time before, her book of poems had been published, dedicated lovingly to George.

She had written some lines that told, better than she knew, of her own strange destiny.

"Sorrow, my friend, when shall you come again?
When shall you come again?
The wind is slow, and the bent willows send
Their silvery motions wearily down the plain. . . .

"Sorrow, my friend,
I owe my soul to you. . . .

CHAPTER EIGHT

For Christ and the Poor

Along the green-bordered path by the Academy of the Assumption Rose Lathrop walked slowly, her red-gold hair burnished in the sunlight of an October afternoon.

For several days the Sisters of Charity and their pupils at the Assumption Academy had watched with interest the convent's noted guest. But they had been careful not to disturb her, for they all knew she had come to Wellesley Hills to make a retreat.

Of course, they could not know that the dignified, yes, even beautiful woman walking so peacefully there along the garden path was fighting the hardest battle of her life. Day by day she faced the tormenting question: what should she do with the rest of her life? It was this intense search for a future, in fact, that had brought Rose to the retreat. Here in the unworldly peace of a prayerful place she hoped to find her answer.

For the first time in her life Rose Lathrop was really alone now. Her father and mother were gone. Una too. Julian had his own family and interests, and the years had come between sister and brother as years will, separating them. Little Francie . . . the ivy-covered grave in Sleepy Hollow, the pure and playful spirit in Heaven . . . that was all! George? He too was lost, in another way, perhaps even sadder than death, for she still loved him, although she knew they could never be together again.

Up to now, Rose had to admit, she had been something of a failure at everything she tried— music, painting, writing—even marriage. She still felt there was something special for her to do. She did not know what, but she had faith. It was about all she did have just then, but it kept telling her that in His way, in His time, God would show her what to do.

Just then, Sister Mary Bernard came down the path to meet Rose.

"I thought I'd find you here, Mrs. Lathrop," she said with a quiet smile. "I wanted to give you this." She handed Rose a small book. Rose read the title as she thanked Sister Bernard. *The Life of St. Vincent de Paul.*

That evening in her small plain room Rose Hawthorne Lathrop took Sister Bernard's book and sat down to read. Night settled very quickly over the convent. After the bell calling the nuns to prayer, hardly another sound disturbed the quiet.

The story of Father Vincent, the French priest who is often called the Father of the Poor, went straight to Rose's heart. She could not set it down until she had finished the last page. She herself felt strongly the desire to help the poor, to relieve suffering in some way. Only a short time before, when asked to give a talk to the New England Women's Press Association in Boston, Rose had surprised them by speaking about Catholic charitable works instead of the life and writings of her father.

Here tonight, in St. Vincent de Paul's life, Rose saw the ideal of charity come alive, compassionate, self-giving, tireless.

"I am for Christ and the poor," Father Vincent had said.

As she put down the book, that motto kept

ringing in Rose's ears. She made a sudden reso-
lution.

"When I go back to New York," she told
herself, "I'll tell the Paulist Fathers that I've
decided to work for the poor. They'll help me
find out just how to do it."

But the answer was not to come so soon.
Father Young encouraged Rose gently, for he
knew that sometimes in the past she had made
sudden decisions on impulse and had been sorry
for them later. Besides, she was a recent con-
vert, full of enthusiasm for her new-found faith.
How lasting would it be?

"Don't forget, Mrs. Lathrop," he would say,
his old eyes kindly above his remarkably long
gray beard, "you haven't been in the Church
very long. A life dedicated to charity brings
many hardships. Let's wait a while and see how
you feel." Perhaps he did not believe the gently bred New England daughter of Hawthorne
really knew what she wanted. Or perhaps it
would be truer to say Father Young did not
yet know all that this determined woman was
capable of doing.

Patience had never been in Rose's nature, but
she had no choice. The winter came and went.
Rose worked hard on the book she was writing
about her father. It was to be called *Memories
of Hawthorne*.

One day she decided to take some of her

clothes to her dressmaker so that they would
be ready to wear when the weather turned
warm again.

She took her yellow silk dress off its hanger
and folded it carefully on top of some others
on her bed. With a little alteration, it would
serve for another season. Yellow was her favorite color.

Putting on her hat and gloves and tying the
dresses in a secure bundle, Rose started out for
the rooming house where her seamstress lived.

She walked along quickly, in her energetic
way, noticing with pleasure that the air was
losing its chill. Yes, spring was on the way. For
just a moment her mind wandered back many
years to a grove of trees on a Concord hillside.
There the wild flowers were beginning to
show green and white, purple and blood-red
through the fallen leaves that formed the forest
floor.

The seamstress lived in a small rented room
in a boarding house. Rose had gone there often
enough before, but this time the landlady
looked very troubled when she opened the door
to Rose's knock.

"Oh no, she's not here any more." The landlady would have closed the door again quickly,
but Rose stepped forward.

"But—would you tell me please where she's
living now? I have some work for her and—"

"She can't work no more, Miss. She's sick.

Very sick." The woman leaned across the threshold and whispered to Rose, "Cancer! I had to get rid of her quick."

"Get rid of her?"

"Yes, sure. Before the other boarders knew what ailed her. They'd all have left me. I have to live, you know." She glanced over her shoulder as if afraid of being overheard by someone inside.

"Where did she go?"

"To the hospital, I guess. But they won't keep her long. She didn't have anything saved up. And she won't get better. I don't know, maybe they sent her to Bellevue." This time the door really did close, leaving Rose still standing on the doorstep.

Rose was stunned. She turned and walked slowly down the stone steps, her bundle of dresses forgotten under her arm.

As she went back along the grimy street, a faint April-like softness cast a sort of brightness even over the plain brown houses. But Rose did not see this. She must find that poor, sick woman, and quickly. She did not know it, but as she started that afternoon to follow the faltering footsteps of the dressmaker, Rose herself was setting forth on a kind of journey from which she was never to return.

The dressmaker was no longer at the hospital the landlady had mentioned. A short note appeared after her name in the admissions book the hospital attendant showed Rose. "Patient's condition worse. Funds exhausted. Patient sent to city hospital."

But she was not at Bellevue either. Here again the record was brief. "Case diagnosed as incurable cancer. Referred to Blackwell's Island."

Rose had never before visited "the Island," a place in the East River that the city kept as a last lonely place of refuge for its sick and poor. Now she hurried to board the ferry that would take her to the grim gray stone building. Perhaps she might still find the poor soul, if only she had come in time!

She did not find her. She was told, when she inquired in the cancer ward of the poorhouse, that the dressmaker had died, and being without money, friend or family, had been buried in the city's graveyard for the abandoned dead!

Down the bleak halls of Blackwell's Island Rose walked. She could hardly believe the new world of misery before her eyes. There were long, long rows of beds. She looked into the drawn pale faces of many who were waiting there to die. Physical pain was deeply drawn on every feature. Yes, and something more was there too. How terrible it would be, Rose thought, to spend one's last days like this, an all-but-nameless stranger among strangers, with-

out even a word of comfort, a single little
token of loving care!

The squat ferry boat chugged fretfully across
the East River back toward Manhattan and
nosed into the pier at the end of 26th Street.
Rose stepped ashore. The cloudy mist that had
hung over the water as she crossed it earlier
had changed now to drizzling rain. On the
dock she saw a strange group gathered waiting
for the next trip. Some crouched in invalid
chairs, some lay on stretchers, some stood hud-
dled together, thin and ragged, looking at
nothing. A white-gowned hospital worker was
with them.

Rose knew they must be cancer patients beyond medical help, being sent by the city authorities to the poorhouse. She had seen too
much that day, and she could not bear to look
as they were silently herded aboard the waiting
ferry for their last trip anywhere.

It was bad enough to have an incurable and
painful illness like cancer. But to be also poor
and friendless, without money to pay doctor's
bills, unwanted even by your own family!

Rose could not put those stricken faces from
her mind. She began to ask questions. What
had happened to the gentle, hard-working
young seamstress must be happening to many
others. Rose went to talk to city and welfare
officials, settlement workers, doctors, nurses.

From all of them she learned the same shocking facts.

Nearly everyone then believed cancer was a contagious disease. And to have it meant at that time certain death. The suffering it brought was beyond description—pain, perhaps disfigurement, a sudden agony or a gradual wasting away. Above all, it brought despair to its victims, horror and revulsion to all who had anything to do with it.

Some doctors even thought that the sooner death came, the better for all. And many of the poor patients felt the same, for if they refused the unkindly shelter of the poorhouse, the only thing left was the street. Or perhaps a damp cellar, hunger, ragged clothing, and the sharp anguish of being an outcast.

Rose knew now what Una had tried to tell her that day many years before when the two girls had stood looking at the children playing in the gutters of a squalid London street.

"Read what Father says about these people," Una had told her, "and you'll never again be able to forget about the poor."

But Rose had not wanted to think of such things then. Poverty was ugly to her. She loved her nice home, flowers, new dresses, music, all that was beautiful.

Now she felt differently. She went to her bookcase and took out *Our Old Home*, the book Hawthorne had written about his life in

England. She turned the pages quickly. Yes,
there was the story.

One day, Hawthorne wrote, someone had
taken him on a visit to a London workhouse.
As he was being shown through the dismal
place by one of the officials, he noticed a little
boy trying to talk to him.

Such a sad-looking child Hawthorne had
never seen before! The poor little face, thin
and white, the body misshapen, the strange
sounds coming from the pale lips, the twisted
hand reaching out and clinging tightly to Hawthorne's coat.

The child could not speak clearly, but there
was no mistaking what he wanted. He was begging the tall handsome visitor to pick him up.
If only for a moment, the orphan wanted to
pretend he belonged to someone.

Rose knew exactly how her father would
have felt at that moment. Even more than she,
Nathaniel Hawthorne had been drawn to beauty,
order, cleanliness, health. These things were easy
to love. Ugliness always saddened and sickened
him. His very sensitive nature made him shy
away from it again and again. Yet this same
sensitive nature had told him that day he must
not ignore the child's pleading. Although it was
probably the last thing on earth he felt like
doing, he had leaned over and gathered the
dirty child in his arms, lifting him up and
carrying him as he went on his way through

the London shelter for the homeless and or-
phaned.

Later on, Hawthorne was able to see a hidden meaning in the unpleasant little incident.
He believed that the child had been there only
to remind him that everyone is in some way
responsible for all the suffering and evil in the
world. We cannot look upon any suffering
person, he had written, even a stranger, as if
his suffering did not concern us too. For we all
share in our brothers' injustice toward another
and must do our best to help him.

Rose closed the book thoughtfully. How
could her father, whose religious views had
been so different from her own, describe so
well a deep Christian truth? Yet he had known
instinctively what it had taken her so long to
discover!

As she placed *Our Old Home* back in its
place on the shelf, another book fell acciden-
tally on the floor. As she reached over to pick
it up, her glance fell upon the opened page.
Again she read her father's word, this time in
The Miraculous Pitcher:

"Human beings owe a debt of love to one
another because there is no other method
of paying the debt of love and care which
all of us owe Providence. . . . Providence
put me here, I hope, among other things
in order that I may make amends for the
inhospitality of my neighbors."

Rose felt as if her father had just spoken directly to her. "To make amends for the inhospitality of my neighbors"—that will be my life from now on, she thought. Rose went down on her knees, crying. She knew what she would do. Her own father had told her. She prayed for help.

All that night, unable to sleep because of the great idea taking shape in her mind, Rose planned how she would go about beginning her hospital for New York's cancerous poor.

First she went to see her friend Josephine Lazarus. After Emma's death from cancer a few years before, Josephine had tried to start some sort of center for the treatment of cancer patients. It was to have been a memorial to her sister.

"But, my dear!" Miss Lazarus was kindly but hardly encouraging. "Of course it's a splendid idea. Only it can't be done. I know, because I tried."

"Why didn't you succeed?" Rose wanted to know.

"Because I couldn't get nurses to look after the patients. Cancer is one illness no one can put up with for long. I offered them the highest pay and hired the best nurses I could find. But they didn't stick to the job."

"I can understand that," Rose answered. She had seen enough by this time to know that not everyone could face cancer.

"It would make Emma very happy, if she were here, to know what you're planning," Miss Lazarus said. "We gave her everything money could provide, yet we had to watch her die. And she was still a young woman. After that I wanted to do something for the less fortunate, those who had to suffer what Emma suffered, but without our love and care to make it more bearable."

"Yes." Rose shook her head sadly. "I remember so well those last few times I came here to see her. Those beautiful dark eyes of hers—how shadowed they were, but she still had her wonderful smile. She thanked me for coming, but we both knew there wouldn't be many more visits."

Rose recalled how hard it had been for her to go into Emma's room and sit down beside the bed. One of the things that made cancer so unbearable was the sickening smell it cast over the room, the bedclothes, anything that came anywhere near the patient.

"If I can't get anyone to help me, I'll do what I can alone," Rose said firmly.

"I wish you every success, Rose," Miss Lazarus said warmly. "I hope it works out. It would be a wonderful work." She took her friend's hand as she prepared to leave. "Let me know when you're ready to begin. I'd like to help with expenses."

CHAPTER NINE

A Door Is Opened

In the big round hospital room a dreadful silence fell. It was time for the daily dressings. Everyone waited to see how the new nurse would stand up before a sight of Mrs. Watson's face—without its mask of bandage.

The nurse in charge worked quickly, impersonally. Rose stood next to her with the tray of supplies.

"Hold this, please!"

Rose put out her hand. The nurse with a deft hand removed the last strip of adhesive. Rose closed her eyes. She had to. Other than that, she did not move. Her hands felt slippery with cold sweat and her head was spinning. She must not fail now, for her future depended upon this moment. And she knew poor Mrs. Watson was watching her closely too, for she knew that her skin cancer was hideous to see.

"Now watch me, please, Mrs. Lathrop, and you'll see how we handle such cases." The nurse's voice was mercifully cool and calm.

With a great effort Rose opened her eyes. It had been less than a minute, but an eternity had passed. Even Mrs. Watson did not guess the shock the new student nurse had just suffered.

When Rose returned to her room that night, her feet burned in the tight-fitting new nurses' shoes and her uniform, so fresh that morning, was rumpled. She closed the door wearily and slipped the stiff shoes from her aching feet. She was tired, more tired than she had ever been before, but somehow she was content. She had taken the first step toward her goal. She had enrolled as a student nurse at the New York Cancer Hospital uptown, facing the west side of Central Park. If she were to devote her life to caring for the sick, then she must know how to do it most effectively.

Each morning she spent on duty at the hospital brought her closer to that purpose. Meanwhile, she lived sparingly, saving every cent she could for greater needs to come.

"And how is everyone feeling today?" she would greet her patients, whose beds formed a sort of circle around the huge room.

She was always sure of at least one cheerful answer. That would come from Mrs. Watson. Ever since the day Rose had steeled herself to this patient's tragedy, a sort of friendship had existed between them. Sickness, the end of a life of hardship, had not dampened the spirits nor dulled the keen wit of this sprightly Irish lady. She never ran out of jokes, and her funny remarks lightened the sufferings of the others in the room.

"Mrs. Watson's circus," Rose would call the ward, for there was a pole going up the center which made it seem very much like a Big Top, with Mrs. Watson, of course, the sole entertainer.

One day Rose's morning greeting went unanswered. She glanced quickly toward Mrs. Watson's corner and saw that the bed was empty. What had happened to her? She certainly was not well enough to go home. In fact, she could never hope to be any better.

Outside in the hall Rose spoke to the nurse in charge. "What's happened to Mrs. Watson?"

"Oh, she was discharged."

"Discharged?" Rose couldn't believe it. "But she's so ill—she needs constant care."

"I know. Her case is hopeless. That's why she had to go. We can't keep patients here once we're sure they're incurable," the nurse explained.

Rose stood still, too shocked to remember what errand she had been on.

"Here, Mrs. Lathrop. This is your clean linen for today."

Automatically, Rose reached out and took the pile of sheets and towels and started back to the ward.

Then she turned quickly to the nurse. "Do you know where she went?"

"We don't know. We were willing to send her to the Island, but she didn't want to go. So—there was nothing more we could do!"

Rose went back and began to change the beds, her mind racing furiously. So Mrs. Watson too had become a victim of the inhuman system that sent the hopeless away to die, always in want, always alone! She must hurry, get this training period over, find a place of her own, and begin her work!

On a hot summer Sunday afternoon Rose took a journey into her future. She went there on a bumping trolley car that took her away from the shaded lawns of Central Park, the fashionable shops of Fifth Avenue, and all the familiar streets of the city of New York.

Down on the East River side of Manhattan Island, far down, was a strange world. It was a crowded crisscross of dingy streets lined with old tenements. Children cried, street vendors manned their pushcarts, and grownups argued in many languages—all in the street.

As she walked along, Rose wondered how people ever lived in conditions like these. She even felt a little frightened here. Then she thought of Una making her way through London slums, and it gave her courage. She began to look more closely at the faces passing by. They were not wicked faces, nor even ugly, though many were thin and drawn from poverty and care. Newcomers from many European countries crowded together here, striving to secure a firmer foothold in the New World. Here Rose had decided to begin her work, for here the need was greatest.

At Number 1 Scammel Street she finally found just what she wanted. Behind its broken wooden fence, the old frame house sagged despondently to one side. Windows gaped jaggedly and the door creaked on its rusty hinges.

Up a rickety staircase, three tiny stuffy rooms opened into one another. They were dark and gloomy, their windows facing a narrow alley. Rose's imagination, once so lively in weaving stories on paper, could see wonders as she looked at the grimy little flat. The building was condemned, so no one else would want it. What was more, the rent was low!

She came at night, for it seemed easier, somehow, with the darkness around her and not so many out to watch the odd new tenant of Number 1. She put up a secondhand iron bed in one of the rooms. Then she lay down to rest, for there was no more to do tonight. She waited for the hubbub of the street to die down, but it never did. Besides that, there was the clatter of horses coming and going at the stable next door. And cats! In the courtyard they seemed to carry on an endless and noisy battle.

Sleep was impossible, but lack of it gave her time to think and plan. In the morning light the place looked even dirtier, but a finger of sunlight stretching in through a dusty window gave her courage. She was down on the floor early with a pail and scrub brush. After that, she bought some paint. She had wanted to be a painter, and now here she was, on hands and knees, painting a tenement floor and getting splinters in her fingers! She made it yellow, the color of marigolds in Concord gardens, her favorite color and one that went well with her gold-red hair.

She painted the outer door and all the walls sparkling white. Corner by corner she chased out the look and smell of age and grime. A few little holy pictures brightened the walls, and a statue of St. Rose, her patron, stood on a table. She had not much furniture, so packing crates would have to do for chairs. With the money she had left she bought a few medical supplies.

Now she was ready to begin. No one could know the doubts and fears she fought in those early days. All we can know is her courage. The neighbors soon grew used to seeing the beautiful lady who walked with such dignity on their littered sidewalk. They knew now why she had come, for patients were already calling at her makeshift clinic.

Sometimes on a stifling evening Rose would walk to the East River nearby for a breath of fresher air. There were the long piers lined with ships, their masts tall and graceful. A faint sea breeze would ruffle her red hair. Somehow the sight of the river had a soothing effect on Rose. Sails and schooners brought back memories of her own ocean voyages. And then, after all, she had come of seagoing people. Later, cooled and refreshed, she would make her way back through knots of playing children to her own small place.

A letter came one day written in a shaky and faint hand.

"Can I come and stay with you?" it asked. It was signed "Mrs. Watson." The message had none of the sparkle and gaiety Rose remembered in its writer.

So far, Rose had lived alone, treating those who came to her during the day or visiting others in their own homes. She welcomed Mrs. Watson as her first "permanent" guest.

"But I can't promise you anything," she warned the old woman. "I'll share with you all I have, but it isn't much."

"It'll be fine, dear. Don't worry," replied Mrs. Watson gratefully, and looking at her, Rose knew that, however little she herself had to offer, it would be more than Mrs. Watson would have elsewhere. Her illness had grown much worse. Rose hardly recognized her, so thin and tired and ragged had she grown in only six weeks! Her relatives would not let her stay with them any longer, and in a way, this was no wonder, for her appearance was frightful. Besides, like so many people, they feared that cancer was contagious. Rose was glad she was going to have the chance to disprove this theory.

"Let me make you a cup of tea, dear." Mrs. Watson, weak as she was, wanted to do everything possible to help Rose. Indeed, after a few days, when Mrs. Watson had quite recovered her old humor and vigor, Rose often felt more like the guest than the hostess.

Mrs. Watson prepared endless cups of tea for Rose that winter, all on an old-fashioned hob

over the fireplace. Rose would scarcely have
survived that first winter without her stricken
friend. Once she was very ill, from overwork
and privation, and Mrs. Watson cared for her
day and night. She told her stories when she
was discouraged, and night after night as Rose
lay ill the old woman knelt beside her to say
the Rosary.

Her faith and patience helped Rose so often
that it was difficult to say which was the benefactor. They nearly forgot that Mrs. Watson's
illness was so soon to take its toll.

But that time had to come. Rose was saddened. She felt she had lost a true friend, one
who had taught her a great deal about love.
There would be many other Mrs. Watsons, she
knew. She prayed that her door would always
stand open to them, and that, when they came,
she might be able to give them perfect love.

Rose couldn't do it alone. Though she was
willing to give her days and nights, her strength
and resources—all she had for the rest of her
life—it still wasn't enough. There were too
many sick people calling on her for help. One
person alone could not care for them all.

Rose had from the beginning faced the fact
that she would find very few helpers. Some
would be willing, she knew, but generosity
would not be enough. Few indeed would ever
possess the physical endurance and spiritual

fortitude needed for the job. She prayed someone would come.

From time to time she had had volunteers,
but they never lasted. This life held little hope
of earthly reward. It offered only the longest
hours, the poorest food, the hardest bed, the
most disagreeable tasks. All that, besides sharing
down to the last misery the thin and ugly lot
of the poor!

It was December 15, 1897. Rose was busy
in the clinic, wondering how long she could
carry on alone. Surely her prayers would be
answered. But when?

She did not know help was already coming,
was in fact just knocking at her door. Alice
Huber put her hand hesitantly to the knocker,
wondering what ever had given her the idea of
coming here. She wished that she were anywhere else—back home in Kentucky with her
parents, or at the art school uptown where she
had been teaching—but here she was, and she
must make the best of it!

A patient waiting her turn for treatment
answered the door, dressed in a strange array of
castoff clothes of different colors. Alice Huber's
eyes quickly took in the cluttered kitchen.

"Is—is Mrs. Lathrop here?" she managed to
ask.

"This way, Miss. In the front room." The
woman motioned through a low doorway.

Alice Huber gathered her neat warm coat

tightly about her and edged between the kitchen table and the ramshackle closet, taking care not to touch anything as she passed.

Her artist's eye saw instantly the one spot of beauty in that drab and sorrow-filled room. Rose, under her cloud of red hair, spoke casually to the guest.

"Just a moment, please. I'll be through in a few minutes. Won't you sit down?"

To sit down in such a place was an effort for the gently bred southern girl. She smoothed her spotless skirt and sat stiffly on the edge of a rickety green sofa worn threadbare with years of use.

Right across from her, an old woman with a witch's face glared at Alice over the top of a walking stick.

"I'm sorry I had to keep you waiting," Rose apologized graciously as soon as she was free.

"I'm Alice Huber," the girl explained. "I read in the paper about your work here."

"Yes—" Mrs. Lathrop seemed to be waiting for her to say something more. Alice pulled an envelope from her purse.

"Father Fidelis sent this letter to introduce me. I believe you know him."

She gave Rose the letter.

"Why yes, I know Father Fidelis well. How kind of him to send you here!" Rose smiled at the remembrance of the tall priest whose con-

version from Anglicanism had created quite a
stir some years before.

"He says that you would like to come and
help us out." The question in Rose's eyes was
very pressing. Alice Huber looked quickly
away.

"Y—yes. I thought maybe—well, I could come
one afternoon a week."

She was sorry she'd said it, but she knew
Rose expected it, and she could not disappoint
her. In the meantime, Alice Huber told herself,
she would find some good excuse not to come.

She tried to put the incident out of her
mind, but the look in Rose's eyes would not
leave her. What kind of woman was this who
could live with such misery, such poverty, and
yet appear so gracious and even cheerful? Over
and over she asked herself that question, and
when Tuesday came, Alice found herself, against
her own will, picking her way cautiously down
the streets of the Lower East Side.

It proved worse than she had expected. She
hated every moment of that afternoon. Me-
chanically she did what Rose asked her to do,
hoping the time would pass quickly so she
could leave. Never again, she told herself, as
she escaped gratefully that evening into the
relatively fresh air of the street!

Again that week the face of Rose Lathrop
haunted her thoughts. That question in her eyes
could not be ignored. Alice Huber knew that

Rose Lathrop needed her, but the older woman would not demand the sacrifice. She realized all too clearly how great it was.

Week after week Alice went back to help out for a few hours. Rose had moved to a place on Water Street, not far from her first location and very much like it in every way, but a little larger.

All her life Rose Lathrop had found it hard to make friends in a purely social way. Now it was her heroism that won the devotion of Alice.

Early in January, hardly three weeks after her first shocking visit to Water Street, Alice told Rose that she had decided to join her for good.

"But I can't come right away because of my teaching assignment," she explained.

Rose could hardly answer. God had answered her prayer for a helper. Alice was a wonderful worker. Her disposition, while very different from Rose's, fitted the situation marvelously. She had many good qualities that Rose lacked, and between them they had all that was necessary for the continuation of the work.

One March night Alice arrived to stay. There was nothing joyous about it. Alice Huber did not feel any glow of self-dedication. Neither then, nor at any time in the long years to come, did she feel any attraction toward what she was to do. Her decision was based on the very matter-of-fact idea that she was needed here, and so she came.

Next morning, very early, the two women went together to Mass at St. Gabriel's Church nearby. It was the great feast of the Annunciation. A Passionist priest, Father Edmund Hill, very kindly offered the Mass for their intention.

A few moments of prayer, then the two women returned to the endless tasks awaiting them. Yet it was a day that would always stand out—the sealing of a lifelong partnership and the official beginning of a great and continuing work for the sick poor.

CHAPTER TEN

The Veil of St. Dominic

The message that called Rose to Roosevelt Hospital was brief and urgent. George was very ill. She must come at once.

A thousand thoughts, a thousand memories came tumbling through her mind as she hurriedly washed her hands and changed into street clothes. Through the kind Paulist Fathers she had heard news of her husband from time to time. Despite poor health he had kept on writing, and some of his work had been quite successful.

Time and again while they were together George had promised to make a new start. Now, as she reached his bedside, she knew that at last he had really done so.

The priest met her at the door, trying to console her.

"George received the Last Sacraments this morning. I talked to him then, and he was ready. He kept his faith to the very end."

"But I—I should have done more. I might have made it easier for him." Rose was overwhelmed with feelings of remorse. If only things had been different!

"You did your best," the priest told her firmly. "You could not have done more. George loved you. That never changed."

"I know." Rose was crying. That chapter of her life, with its human joys and disappointments, was closed forever. She put into her purse George's prayerbook, its ribbons marking his favorite passages.

Sadly she returned to Water Street. There, in the cramped waiting room, two new patients waited for her. Rose, putting her personal suffering as far back in her mind as possible, began to make ready the bandages for others' wounds.

Each morning Rose would take her kit of dressings and medicines and set off in her plain nurse's dress to make her rounds. For there were some too sick to come to her tiny clinic, and these must be cared for at home. Sometimes, if she had any money, she would stop at a fruit stand or bake shop to buy a little treat for the shut-ins on her list.

Then she would pick her way up and down strange streets trying to find the number she had jotted on a scrap of paper in her pocket. As she knocked at the door, she had to brace herself, for she never knew what she would find inside. Sometimes her patient would be lying on something much more like a bundle of old rags than a bed, in a room cluttered and dusty, and everywhere the terrible smell of illness and neglect.

To these miserable places Rose brought, besides nursing skill, hope, consolation, and the knowledge that someone cared.

"You're an angel—that's what you are!" the aged Mrs. Daly said in her soft Irish voice as she looked up from her bed one morning to see Rose walking in. Rose smiled warmly as she set down her bag and prepared to go to work. First she put a pan of water on the rickety stove and then, while waiting for that to heat, she began tidying up the tenement flat.

Mrs. Daly lay back weakly as Rose straightened the bed, plumped the sagging pillows, and then pared some vegetables for stew, thinking of the other calls she must make, thinking of Alice trying to handle alone all the patients that came daily to Water Street.

After she left, the old woman dozed off. Usually she had no other visitors, but today young Father Thuente came by. His duties as parish visitor for St. Vincent Ferrer's Church had brought him here before.

"Why, what's happened here, Mrs. Daly?" he asked, looking around the shabby room. "Looks neat as a pin here. Don't tell me you've been up housecleaning?"

"No, it's my angel who did it, Father," said the sick woman. And she told him of the mysterious red-haired woman who came every few days to care for her.

"But who is she?" Father wanted to know.

"Bless us, I don't even remember her name, though I know she told it to me. Oh, I have it here someplace. She wrote it down for me in case I need her in a hurry—" She ruffled through some odds and ends on her cluttered table. "Here it is." She drew out a torn scrap of paper.

Father Thuente took it and read the name.

"Mrs. Lathrop, 668 Water Street."

Who was this woman, and why was she devoting her time to visiting people like Mrs. Daly? He made up his mind to find out.

Standing before the Water Street address a few days later, Father Thuente wondered if he had made a mistake. If he had expected the cold bare entrance to a social service bureau, he couldn't have been more disappointed. The shaky old frame house was in pitiable condition, and Father really wondered if it were safe to risk the stairs. But he did. At the top, the trail of the mysterious Mrs. Lathrop became plainer, for there was a clean white door with a knocker that seemed to invite all passers-by.

It was Rose herself who opened the door.

"I'm Father Thuente," the priest explained, "one of the Dominicans of St. Vincent Ferrer's Church on 65th Street. And you, I believe, must be Mrs. Daly's angel!" He smiled as he stepped inside and looked around.

"It's kind of you to come and see us, Father," Rose was saying with her most gracious manner. "We're a little crowded here, as you see, but—"

What Father saw answered many questions that had been in his mind: the plain room, brightened with paint by loving hands, its corners shiny, its occupants all wearing the look of pain and the patience of the poor; on one wall a small figure of the Blessed Mother, reverently arranged; on the table a picture of St. Rose, a Dominican like himself.

After that visit, Father Thuente returned to Water Street again and again. Gradually he

learned Rose's story and became a faithful
friend. Later he was named official spiritual
advisor there and was helpful in settling the
many problems that arose as the work ex-
panded.

By this time, Rose and Alice saw clearly the
need for some sort of organization in their
work. "We would like to be known as the
Servants of Relief for Incurable Cancer," Rose
told Father. She wished very much they could
wear some special dress to identify them, partic-
ularly in the worst neighborhoods they visited.
"I've asked Archbishop Corrigan for permission
to wear some kind of religious habit," she said,
"but he does not feel the time has come for that.
Perhaps later he'll say yes, but—"

Rose had never been noted for her patience.
This time Father Thuente had a suggestion.

"I think St. Dominic would approve of your
work here without a doubt," he told the two
women. "Have you ever considered becoming
members of the Dominican Third Order? After
all, your patron, St. Rose, was a Tertiary."

"Do you think the Archbishop would allow
it?" asked Rose excitedly.

"If you agree, I'll speak to him myself,"
said the priest.

The good news came quickly. They were to
be received as Tertiaries immediately, though

they could not yet wear the white habit of St. Dominic.

Rose and Alice were greatly encouraged.

"And you, of course, will take the name of St. Rose when we are received," Alice said.

Rose answered firmly, in her most determined voice.

"No, I've already thought of that. You must take the name of our patron. You deserve it more than I."

"But then what name will you take?" Alice knew it was useless to protest one of Rose's decisions.

"I've been reading the life of St. Alphonsus Liguori," Rose explained. "You know, he led a very worldly life until one day he happened to visit a hospital for the incurably ill. The sight of these poor people made him resolve instantly to spend the rest of his life caring for them."

So it was decided. At the simple ceremony of their reception as Tertiaries of St. Dominic, Rose Lathrop and Alice Huber became Sister Mary Alphonsa and Sister Mary Rose.

Their rules were few, but never to be broken. First, no patient was to be used for medical experiments of any kind. Second, no patient must ever be made to feel that his illness had made him ugly to look at or repulsive to touch.

"And, in cases of external cancers, we'll

never wear rubber gloves when dressing wounds," Sister Alphonsa declared, "for this would show fear of disease."

The last rule was that no money must be accepted either from the patients themselves or from their relatives or friends.

People were now beginning to hear strange stories of the Sister Alphonsa's work. Newspaper reporters came down to Water Street to see if it were really true that Hawthorne's daughter could be seen there daily nursing the cancerous poor.

Sister Alphonsa did not care for publicity for herself, yet she noticed that each newspaper account brought a welcome response in contributions—money, food, clothing—and some readers even came to offer their services.

"You know, Sister Rose," she said one evening as the two friends sipped their cups of tea after the last patient had gone to sleep. "I think if more people knew about us, they would be glad to help. There are so many generous souls in the world."

Sister Rose nodded. It had been through a news story that she herself had first heard of the work. Later that same night, during the brief hours when Water Street enjoyed a relative quiet and peace, Sister Alphonsa sat down at her table and drew out a sheet of notepaper. She took up her pen thoughtfully. Her idea was a simple one. The more people heard of her work, the more help she would get. So, quite directly, she would tell everyone what she was trying to do.

Sister Alphonsa was tired now, and this was her only chance to sleep. Yet, even as the moments of the night ticked away, some other unknown sufferer waited through the darkness to knock at her door. Thinking of this stranger so soon to be seeking her aid, Sister Alphonsa began to write.

How she wrote! Night after night, she turned out letters to newspapers, letters to relatives, friends, acquaintances, to anyone at all who had shown a passing interest in her efforts. After the letters came articles, stories, advertisements, appeals of every kind, some of which were published in daily papers and magazines, and some of which appeared later in her own little publication called *Christ's Poor*.

The name of Hawthorne worked magic with the editors to whom she addressed her appeals. Always friendly to her because of her father's reputation, they were glad to publish everything she sent. Help came pouring in, wonderful gifts of many kinds.

Sister Alphonsa had already begun taking in patients who had no other place to stay. One by one they came to her and she could not turn them away. "We must have a hospital,"

she said to Sister Rose. "They have no other
place to go."

"Our space is so limited and already so
crowded," replied Sister Rose. One by one, cots
were pushed into this corner and that, every
bit of wall space being used until the tiny flat
seemed ready to burst.

"We'll have to have a bigger place," Sister
Alphonsa decided. "People are sending us do-
nations in every day's mail."

She began to plan a move to larger quarters.
Soon she had found a house in nearby Cherry
Street, an old run-down building but still much
better suited to their needs.

"We can put twelve patients here," Sister
Alphonsa said happily. In her mind she was
already arranging the beds—this way, that way—
to give the best light, the most sun, and most
of all, the privacy so often denied to the very
poor.

The next thing Sister Rose knew, Sister
Alphonsa was busily ordering potted palms and
an awning.

"For the roof garden!" she announced tri-
umphantly.

Puzzled, Sister Rose went up and looked
again at the roof. Perhaps it did have possibilities, she thought, but they would never have
occurred to anyone except the resourceful Sister
Alphonsa. Under the shade of the awning a

few chairs could be placed, and—yes, it would make a lovely spot for the patients to sit.

Though the street just below was anything but lovely, the view from the roof swept the East River, the shiny new Brooklyn Bridge, and the ships that stood restlessly at their piers. Up there the air was light and the sun golden, the sky New York's own electric blue.

That is how St. Rose's Home began.

Soon they had their twelve patients, but it did not stop there. More kept coming, and once again Sister Alphonsa began to dread the hesitant knocks upon her door. In each one she seemed to hear the trembling hand of the poor seamstress whose tragedy she had learned too late. It wasn't taking them in that was hard; it was turning them away.

News of the happenings on Cherry Street was coming often to Archbishop Corrigan. He began to lose the caution with which the Church officially regards such new ventures. Far from being merely a short-lived idealistic dream, St. Rose's Home was now an established institution. The care of the incurably ill was surely a divine mission.

In the small chapel at St. Rose's, Mass was celebrated once each week. Those who were able came to kneel before the simple altar. Sister Alphonsa opened the doors of adjoining sickrooms so that those who could not come to

the altar might be present too. It was thrilling
to her to kneel there as Father Thuente, ac-
companied by Sister Rose carrying a lighted
candle, went from room to room bringing Holy
Communion to the bedsides of Catholic patients.

One day Father Thuente came with wonderful news.

"I've spoken to the Archbishop again," he
told them. "He has given permission for you
both to make your religious professions as
Sisters of St. Dominic."

Sister Alphonsa and Sister Rose were jubilant.
Now they were to exchange the semireligious
dress they had been wearing for the white habit
of St. Dominic.

The ceremony took place on December 8,
the Feast of the Immaculate Conception. The
two women who had worked so valiantly together knelt side by side and pronounced their
first vows to the priest who had been their
spiritual benefactor. Several other girls who had
come to join the community were there too.

Perhaps the occasion was a little less elaborate
than a Solemn Profession generally is, but that
did not lessen the joy in Sister Alphonsa's heart.
The sermon, though somewhat hurried, was
beautiful, and, after all, on this day as well as
all others the needs of the sick came first.

As Sister Alphonsa hurried down the hall,
feeling a bit stiff and strange in her new habit,

the veil falling softly over her shoulders to hide the glorious red hair that had made her so striking, she knew that at last restless Rose Hawthorne had found happiness.

CHAPTER ELEVEN

Haven on a Hill

Outside the small railroad station of Unionville, Gustave waited. It would be hard to say which looked saddest—Gustave, his wagon, or his horse. They were all three very old.

Gustave took out his polka-dot kerchief and mopped his brow, though it was only May and the sun just pleasantly warm.

Then he climbed down from the wagon and patted the tired-looking horse.

"What's to become of us, François?" he muttered, half to himself. "Now that the Fathers are leaving the hill, going off to China—"

He gave the animal a smart rap on the side. "Nuns! Well, as long as they're coming, might as well get a bit spruced up for them, I suppose."

From under the driver's seat he drew a tattered rag and began to polish the harness and bridle. They too had seen better days. Then he dusted the seats of the wagon, for he remembered that the nuns would be wearing white habits.

By that time the train was whistling. It came roaring along beside the station. Gustave limped off to see if he could find the nuns. It was not at all hard to spot them, alighting from the steps of the train.

"The Fathers sent me," Gustave explained briefly. "Wagon's out this way."

He led the way back to the broken-down vehicle standing outside.

"It's not so comfortable, Sisters," the old man added rather apologetically. "Seen a lot of service—me and it."

"It's quite all right," Sister Alphonsa smiled. If only he knew what they had just come from, he wouldn't apologize, she thought. Why, even to breathe in the fresh country air with spring in it, a fragrance nearly wiped from her memory by life on Water Street! She and Sister

Rose would have been quite satisfied to walk to Sherman Park.

"Of course, we're only going to look at it!" said Sister Rose firmly, glancing around at her companion.

"Of course!" agreed Sister Alphonsa.

She knew as well as anyone that they certainly couldn't afford to buy a house in the country, much as they needed one. Still, when the Sherman Park Dominicans invited them to come up and see the place, she thought they shouldn't refuse.

They creaked along up the steep road. How many trips, wondered Gustave, had he and François made up that particular hill?

Behind him, Sister Alphonsa and Sister Rose lifted their tired eyes and saw the house. The fresh green of new leaves surrounded them and the scent of violets brought back Concord springtimes.

One of the French Fathers showed Sister Alphonsa and Sister Rose around the house. Proudly he pointed out the orchard he had planted, his beehives, a grape arbor. There were greenhouses full of flowers and beds laid out in the garden. Behind the house was a grove of trees—oak, beech, maple. Best of all, Sister Alphonsa could look out over the valley, across the pale blue hills of Westchester that met the sky on either side. Before that lovely view Sister Alphonsa felt her good sense wavering. Her firm decision "just to look, not to buy" seemed foolish indeed!

Down at St. Rose's Home, in the hand of the St. Joseph statue in the chapel, the statue before which Rose so often prayed, was a tiny note written in her own firm script: "Glorious St. Joseph, please give to the Servants of Relief a house in which they can take care of many sick in safety for many years."

She thought of all the poor sick men and women who might come up here and spend their last days amid beauty and peace. But Sister Rose was there to bring her back to earth abruptly.

"How could we ever pay for it?" inquired her practical companion.

Sister Alphonsa frowned and her voice had a sharp edge as she answered: "What a thing to say!"

"The house is old, Sister," Father explained. "It's not the latest thing, but it would be wonderful for a hospital. It has sixty rooms."

At this poor Sister Rose almost fainted. Sixty rooms! How could their tiny group of Sisters care for all that, and the patients too? As a monastery, the place looked cold and bare. Sister Alphonsa mentally made notes on how to change that. Flowers, pictures, a bit of color here, rockers on the long porches—why, the place would be actually cosy!

"But we could only give you a thousand

dollars now, Father," Sister Alphonsa heard herself saying. She was afraid even to look toward Sister Rose.

"That's fine, Sister. You can pay the rest whenever you are able. We'll be glad to leave the place in your hands when we go to the missions."

The price of the house and grounds, livestock and view, was $28,000. Sister Alphonsa did not know until later that the cost also included Gustave, François and their aged wagon.

He was so happy not to have to leave! Right away he seemed to grow about twenty years younger. He gave the wagon a good polishing and took François down to the station to meet the first patients. Up the hill they toiled, past the Lourdes grotto, through the big wide gate that was never closed. The air was fragrant with peach blossoms and the rocking chairs were in place on the porch.

On the Feast of Corpus Christi, Rosary Hill Home was officially opened with a High Mass. Gustave bought himself a new kerchief with bright polka dots. He now had so many things to do he quite forgot he had ever felt lonely and forgotten.

That winter the winds blew high. They blew cold. They made the old house grumble and shiver. They made the water pipes freeze and the coal run out faster than Mother Alphonsa

could pay for it. They made the hands of the
Sisters red and raw from overwork. Very often
there was not enough money to pay the bills.
Only prayer would make help come in time.

The patients never knew the Sisters were
having such a hard time of it. For them everything was the best—food, clothing, even those
little comforts that, while unnecessary, add so
much to the happiness of the ill. One look at
their eyes as they rocked contentedly on the
porch or walked around the grounds under the
trees, and Mother Alphonsa could not doubt
she had done the right thing in coming to
Rosary Hill.

Then people began to come to the rescue.
Rose had never given up writing of her work,
of the needs of her "family." She had been
publishing her little magazine, *Christ's Poor*.
Famous and wealthy persons were coming to the
aid of Rose who, as Superior of the growing
community, was now known as Mother Alphonsa. Some left legacies for the work. The
noted writer, Mark Twain, sent a letter of
warm support, and his wife later donated some
much-needed items to the Home. George M.
Cohan, whose music had put smiles into the
hearts of many, gave a benefit concert for the
Sisters. Dr. James J. Walsh, Catholic physician,
scholar, writer and generous benefactor, continued to give public lectures for the benefit of
the Home. And many friends from earlier days,

from Concord and New London, even from the Greenwich Village Friday nights offered help.

At Wayside, a big celebration was being planned in 1904. It was the 100th anniversary of Nathaniel Hawthorne's birth. Mother Alphonsa was, of course, invited to be present and to give a lecture on her memories of her father. She had to reply that she could not spare the time, nor did she feel capable of giving an address for the occasion. She would try to recall something for them in her letter. Writing it took her back many years, and Mother Alphonsa realized fleetingly that she herself was no longer young. Floods of memories crowded her little convent room. Again it seemed that her father was near, with his wonderful smile, his deep resonant voice.

When old Gustave had first driven the nuns through the town of Sherman Park on errands for the Home, some of the residents shook their heads doubtfully, wondering whether the strangers on the hill were bringing disease into their pleasant community. They soon learned this was not so, and as years passed they grew used to the silent procession of the sick up the hill road.

It was not long after the Sisters' arrival that the town fathers decided to change the name of their community to Hawthorne. "It's in honor of my father," Mother Alphonsa would say, never thinking it was really a tribute to

her. She looked for no reward except to hear
her guests exclaim on their arrival at Rosary
Hill, "This is Heaven!"

Sometimes they expressed their gratitude in
touching ways. On the feast of St. Alphonsus
one year, all the men patients joined in sending
Mother a splendid letter of greeting. The spelling was odd, but the thoughts were ever so sincere. Mother Alphonsa had tears in her eyes as
she read it. Such words wiped away all the
hardships of those years.

In December of 1909 the Golden Jubilee of
the Immaculate Conception was being celebrated
throughout the world. This great feast had a
special meaning for Mother Alphonsa and for
Sister Rose, for it was exactly nine years since
they had received the habit and pronounced
their first vows in their little chapel down on
Cherry Street. Now they made their final vows.
This time there were other nuns of their community kneeling around them, some of them
novices being trained in the religious life.

In those nine years they had received around
one thousand patients. No one had ever been
refused who possessed the two qualifications for
admission: empty pocketbook and incurable
cancer. Nearly all of them had died at the
Homes, either in New York or Rosary Hill,
but some had lived to quite an age despite their
sickness.

Still, there were others for whom there was no room. At Rosary Hill it was always possible to fit one more in, sometimes in a chair temporarily, or in a bed heroically donated by someone less seriously afflicted. At St. Rose's in the city, the walls were bursting and many who came there were too sick to take the trip all the way to Rosary Hill. For them a larger hospital was needed.

A sum of $25,000 had been offered by a family in New York toward a new building, if Mother Alphonsa could raise an equal amount. Twenty-five thousand dollars was a staggering sum for a woman who could scarcely pay her guests' grocery bills, but she was not discouraged. She had, in fact, already picked the site where the new St. Rose's would some day stand. It lay at Front and Jackson Streets, near the East River, in view of the Brooklyn Navy Yard. Mother Alphonsa had secretly planted a medal of St. Joseph there, so it was as good as hers! Besides, this spot was very dear to her. She remembered coming here often for a breath of air in the early days.

She would have fifty beds, she planned. She prayed to St. Joseph. At last a generous man named Cornelius Cronin offered the other $25,000. Immediately the land was bought, the plans drawn, and the old buildings torn down.

It rose quickly, a neat red building, and when it was ready, Cardinal Farley came to

bless it. Mother Alphonsa looked around, and
everything she saw made her happy. All was
shiny and new. The beds stood waiting. The
patients would be brought in at once, for they
too had waited and prayed.

Time at Rosary Hill passed quickly. The
first World War had come and gone, but the
Hudson waters flowed on patiently at the foot
of Mother Alphonsa's hill. Her roses blossomed,
pink and fragrant. Her community grew, and
the patients kept coming.

One day a different kind of caller came, a
dignified man well along in years, but still erect
and firm of step. It was Julian Hawthorne, the
brother from whom years and differences had
separated Mother Alphonsa. The two sat together and looked out over the countryside,
taking as gently as possible the measure of what
life had done to each.

Julian had written many books. He had a
large family. The quarrels that had once come
between them seemed very unimportant.

"Do you remember that day in the Corso—"

"Oh yes, and the druid-stones on the Isle of
Man—"

Back and forth, weaving again the web of
years. They laughed, recalling the amusing
scenes of their childhood.

Julian turned from the peaceful valley spread
before him and looked at his sister. Yes, it was

certainly Rose. The lively gray eyes he remembered, the impetuous ways. These were not hidden by the religious habit she wore.

"You are truly happy, aren't you, Rose?" he asked at last.

"I've found my work, Julian. Yes, I'm happy."

"And your faith—you've never regretted becoming a Roman Catholic?" Julian himself had never felt the need of any formal religion. Later on he wrote a magazine article about his sister, whom he admired even though he did not quite understand her.

"Doesn't it seem a pity," he asked in his story, "that one so well suited to give pleasure to the world should wish to confine herself to the poorest and most barren of human creatures?"

He answered his own question.

"Such persons have learned . . . things which we do not know. They have felt a joy and seen a beauty in which we cannot believe, for which they would not exchange the kingdoms and glory of all the earth. . . .

"It is vain to argue with such persons; but, if you examine them narrowly, you may find upon their hands and feet the marks of the nails."

CHAPTER TWELVE

St. Joseph Keeps His Trust

"It isn't my idea at all," Mother Alphonsa kept saying, as the day of the Silver Jubilee drew near.

"But it's twenty-five years now, Mother, since your work began. Don't you think it's time for a celebration?" Father Thuente was smiling, but he was also firm.

Mother Alphonsa grudgingly had to agree, though she never liked praise. She remembered almost as clearly as yesterday that day down at

Cherry Street when Father had received Sister
Rose and herself as members of the Third
Order of St. Dominic.

On the fourteenth of September, the day
chosen for the Jubilee, Rosary Hill was all in
bloom. Early in the day friends began to gather,
to crowd the little chapel. Mother Alphonsa took
her place quietly. Father Thuente, she thought,
was probably going to say a good many things
about her that weren't quite so. But he had insisted on giving the sermon, so what could she
do? She was listening with only half an ear.

It was a very nice day for her. She always
enjoyed having friends come. She liked to show
them around, pointing out an addition here, a
change there, or a flower she especially liked.
A band played on the lawn and tables were
laid for lunch under the trees.

Someone had handed Mother Alphonsa a
note. It was from her friends the Smiths, and
she opened it as she stood talking to Father
Thuente. They were sorry they would be unable to attend the celebration. Mother Alphonsa
read the note quickly, showed it to Father, re-
folded the paper and started to put it back into
the envelope. It wouldn't go in. She fumbled
with it; maybe her fingers were getting stiff.

"Oh, it's too bad they couldn't be here," she
was saying to Father, "but—what's this?" A
small blue slip fluttered out of the envelope.

She unfolded it and silently handed it to Father.

A check for $50,000!

"Thank God for this!" she said softly. "It's the foundation for our new building."

Time sped on, and the needs grew with the number of patients. The new St. Joseph's was no longer adequate. A hospital big enough for a hundred patients must be built and the nuns also needed a new home.

Mother Alphonsa had to raise the money. Again her campaign went into full swing. This consisted quite simply of sitting down at her desk and writing. Letters to friends, letters to newspapers, letters to strangers, letters to everyone and anyone who would be likely to help. It reminded her of that story of her father's she had always loved so much, *The Miraculous Pitcher*, but in this case it was her letters that were an endless source of hospitality for the needy stranger knocking at her door.

Sometimes she would send off another kind of letter to an old friend she had never seen— Brother Joseph Dutton, for many years carrying on the work Father Damien had begun for the leprosy victims of Molokai.

"Beloved Brother"—she would begin, and then her pen would pause as the picture came to mind. A mountainous island far off in the glistening Pacific. A white-bearded old man, sitting at a tiny writing desk in a small bare

room in the stillness of a tropic night, the
statue of St. Joseph faithfully standing guard
on the shelf over his head. She knew the scene
well, for Brother Dutton had sent her snap-
shots, as well as little gifts for her patients,
small pink shells from Molokai Beach, religious
mementos made of Hawaiian flowers.

Once she had even asked Brother Dutton to
come to New York and start a brotherhood to
care for cancer-stricken men. The answer had
been brief. Brother Dutton never could make
words say exactly what he wanted them to, but
he felt he was too old to start a new work.
Besides—and Mother Alphonsa must have
known this—he had promised long ago to stay
at Molokai the rest of his life.

It was July 8, 1926. The League of Nations
was just six years old. In ten months the soli-
tary young adventurer named Charles Lind-
bergh would take off in "The Spirit of St.
Louis" for Orly Airport in Paris on the first
solo non-stop ocean flight in history.

On Broadway, the first talking film, *The
Jazz Singer*, starring Al Jolson, was advertised
in bright lights. A young Kansas-born Army
officer reported for further military training—
Lieutenant Colonel Dwight D. Eisenhower, destined to become the thirty-fourth President of
the United States.

History had moved fast and the world had changed much since the child Rose Hawthorne had played under quiet Concord's spreading trees.

At Rosary Hill it was a warm summer night. The village of Hawthorne lay quietly below in the darkness. Mother Alphonsa's guests were resting, more or less peacefully. Here and there was heard a flurry of quick steps as a nun in white went to one of the beds.

In Mother Alphonsa's small plain room the lamp burned brightly as the Superior sat writing letters. She felt stronger than she had in some time, which made her glad, for she never seemed to get all her letters written. There was always one more person to be thanked, one more begging note to be sent.

Her pen scratched faintly along the pale thin sheet of paper. Her writing, fine and delicate, showed firmness. Behind her gracious phrases was more than a hint of unshakable conviction. She did not aim these days at literary style.

"I never really wanted to write about life," she had said. "I wanted to live it."

Her face, thoughtful as she wrote, was clear and hardly lined. Still a beautiful face, only gently touched by time. Her gray eyes were still keen. Mother Alphonsa had just passed her seventy-fifth birthday. She had never liked to speak about her own past, and now few people ever thought about it. Yet in her letters she drew a vivid picture of herself.

Dr. James J. Walsh, a prominent physician and scholar who had been for many years a constant benefactor, once asked Mother Alphonsa a direct question. She sent back a direct answer.

"What do we do for our sick, in their darkest moments? . . . What you do yourself, when you attend a poor person, abandoned by those who should care for him and suffering from a most humiliating and painful disease.

"You take the hand which no one else had a desire to touch, and you press it, as you say that God will bless them in the next life in just so far as they have suffered bravely and resignedly in this world!"

Hands no one else wanted to touch! How many of these had she soothed in pain and folded in death? She had lost count long ago. More than food and shelter, more even than medicine and nursing care, Mother Alphonsa's gift to her patients was the consolation of being loved and the knowledge that death is not the final tragedy.

"Why, I may die sooner than any of you!" she had often said cheerfully, and the thought seemed to give them wonderful encouragement. Once accepted, the fact of death, no more partial to them than to other mortals, lost much of its terror.

In its place came peace, bringing a vast enjoyment of little things—a cup of tea, a flower, a bird's note, a walk beneath autumn-bright branches.

Some people thought at times that Mother Alphonsa was a bit too indulgent of her patients' whims. Satisfying them often cost money, and there was hardly enough of that! Still, on her shopping tours to the city, Mother Alphonsa was likely to spend more on special comforts than on necessities. Once she came back with a set of fine china, light and frail as the flowers painted on them.

"They are lovely, Mother," exclaimed one of the Sisters, somewhat doubtfully, "but they wouldn't last any time with the hard wear we give dishes here!"

Mother Alphonsa smiled a little sheepishly. "I hope they won't give you too much trouble in the kitchen, Sister, but you know, I've noticed some of our women aren't eating very well. Maybe our heavy cups and plates discourage hands that aren't too strong. I thought this china might make them feel more like eating the good food you prepare for them."

The community never knew what Mother Alphonsa would come home with next. The Sister who went with her on her shopping trips always came back exhausted, but Mother Alphonsa would be jubilant over the thought of making some patient happy. Once she even bought a small radio for one of the men to make the hours pass more quickly. Another time it was a pair of Australian doves. "They're for Helen and Charlotte," she explained, indicating two children who had come to stay at Rosary Hill. They had fun with the chickens and ducks, and Helen was especially fond of canaries.

"Here's Jack and here's Jill, two new playmates for you," Mother Alphonsa told the girls. The delight in their faces was quite enough to repay her for her trouble.

For those who came to spend their last days or years with her, Mother Alphonsa wanted everything to be as pleasant as possible. There was never any hint of a grim institutional regimen. Patients felt free to do whatever pleased them within the limits of their strength, and the house itself, the grounds around it—even the hilltop with its sweeping view of Westchester Valley—all were beautiful. Even if the outer or inner wounds of their disease could not be healed, those caused by poverty, neglect and bitterness disappeared like magic at Rosary Hill.

It was, in fact, quite possible to be happy again, and many of them were. Why not, for never again would they have worries or cares! "The doom of an incurable," Mother Alphonsa had written, "doesn't make us careless of life or happiness for them. . . . So they live, as a rule, quite as long as anyone should wish to do, who believes in Heaven."

Outside the window on this summer evening, the concrete mixers rested, gawky shapes in the shadows. In the morning the workmen would come again to feed them sand and concrete and pails of water. The walls of the new hospital would rise higher and higher. It was coming along fast, but not fast enough for Mother Alphonsa. She could already see its one hundred beds neatly made up with sparkling linen, and, of course, fresh flowers every day at each shrine, in every room—flowers she had tended herself because they gave such happiness to her guests.

"Sorrow, my friend, I owe my soul to you!"
Written long ago in disillusion, the line had now a ring of triumph. For her the saving sorrow had been that of the lonely, the sick, the poor.

How she had once longed for success and recognition! But each ambition only brought another disappointment. Now she had praise, medals, an honorary college degree, magazine articles extolling her accomplishments. None of them meant so much to her as the unfinished foundation outside.

Lately everyone was telling her to stop working, to stop writing, to rest. She had promised, over and over, but there was always one more thing she must see to. Not that she wasn't tired! Sometimes she found it hard to go on, but if her strength failed, her enthusiasm was as bright as ever. She had written not long ago to Sister Rose, "Soon, soon I shall rest."

But she hadn't been quite ready—yet.

In another part of the rambling house the youngest novice of Rosary Hill was sleeping, lightly, and not too well. She was not yet used to the convent bed or to the bell that wakened her early every morning. She had been there only a few days, brought from New York by Sister Rose.

"Why, Mother," Sister Rose had exclaimed in surprise as she saw the Superior opening the door, "why did you come down to meet us? We could have come up to you."

"Not come down!" Mother Alphonsa was almost indignant. "Do you think I would miss being here to welcome you?"

She looked at the girl who stood somewhat shyly on the step, wearing her white high school graduation dress.

"Come—come in, my dear. How pretty you look!"

Strong arms, strong heart, and above all, that spark of heroism! Young as she looked, this teenager had them. With others like her, the work of the Servants of Relief would go on.

The gate at the foot of the hill would always stand open.

Now she came to the end of the last letter. With an effort she signed her name, "Mother Alphonsa Lathrop," the well known signature that seemed to sum up the past and present.

She got up stiffly, for she had been sitting still a long time. On a corner of the table was her sewing basket, with the stockings she had darned for the Sisters, all finished and ready to be given out, as usual, on Saturday night.

She gathered the sheaf of letters together and went out into the silent hall. The perfume of the flowers met her, a soft presence through the house. A breeze stirred the branches against the boarded walls. She thought of her old friends the pigeons, sleeping softly under the eaves of the endless porches. Their low voices were still now, but they had often been company for her in lonely days when her work was young.

It was after ten o'clock.

Sister Mary Francis was coming toward her in the hall, her skirts rustling softly. "Why Mother, you still working? You look so tired! Why don't you go straight to bed?"

"Yes. Yes, Sister. I'm going now, I promise."

First she would go to the chapel, for her evening visit, the last few minutes that seemed to set all the happenings of the day straight.

She went in and left her letters with a prayer
at St. Joseph's statue. In the morning they
would be mailed.

Now at last Mother Alphonsa could rest.

AFTERWARD

Today, through early detection, skillful surgery, and the use of radium, one-third of all cancer patients—150,000 each year—are saved, an attainment undreamed of when Rose Hawthorne Lathrop began her work. New and hopeful advances in cancer treatment are constantly being reported.

Meanwhile the Servants of Relief for Incurable Cancer continue their mission of caring for those cases beyond medical help. They work in seven hospitals in seven cities: Hawthorne, New York; Philadelphia, Pennsylvania; Fall River, Massachusetts; Atlanta, Georgia; St. Paul, Minnesota; Parma, Ohio. As this story was being written, another St. Rose's Home opened its doors on New York's Lower East Side. If you visit one of these Homes you will find amidst so much suffering a wonderful spirit of peace, and sometimes laughter and singing.

History has a way of drawing together events

widely separated in space and time. In this case
the trail winds all the way from Gallows Hill
in Salem to the feet of St. Joseph's statue in a
convent chapel. We may even say that the
mysterious pilgrimage begun by Nathaniel Hawthorne and finished by Rose came to an end
here. Yet it has not really ended while the Servants of Relief continue their work.

At Rosary Hill you may see Rose Hawthorne's engagement and wedding rings on the
hand of the Infant of Prague statue. But a
better memento of her may be found in the
words engraved on the cornerstone of the hospital she built: "This is her last gift to the poor.
May her name be held in everlasting remembrance."

VISION BOOKS